AN END TO PROMISES

AN END
TO PROMISES

Sketch of a Government 1970-74

DOUGLAS HURD

Collins
St James's Place, London
1979

William Collins Sons & Co Ltd
London · Glasgow · Sydney · Auckland
Toronto · Johannesburg

First published 1979
© Douglas Hurd 1979

ISBN 0 00 216031 5

Set in Monotype Times Roman
Made and Printed in Great Britain by
William Collins Sons & Co Ltd, Glasgow

CONTENTS

Acknowledgement is due to the Daily Telegraph *for permission to reproduce on page 91 an extract from an article by Mr T. E. Utley.*

INTRODUCTION

Two years ago I wrote a novel about Number Ten Downing Street, and thought that would be enough. For a time it was; but recently the thought of another book about working in that house has been nagging at my mind. *Vote to Kill* perhaps caught the flavour of Number Ten as an institution – the way people talk, tea is made, papers flow, the tension of private and public lives mingles in the same building. But invented characters are no substitute for real ones. Fiction set vaguely fifteen years ahead is no substitute for the actual years 1970–4. Already the myths are growing, the subtleties are being lost, and the flavour is escaping.

This book is not a history of Mr Heath's premiership. It is too soon for that; nor am I qualified to write it. I have consulted no government documents. I have interviewed no high personages. There are many papers which I never saw, meetings which I did not attend, motives and explanations at which I can only guess. I have simply tried to set down something of what I saw, did and felt as the Prime Minister's Political Secretary during those years.

This limitation has, I realize, turned what follows into something of a ragbag. The length at which the book deals with a subject is a measure of my involvement in that subject, not of its importance. For example, I mention Ulster only in passing, yet it was the gravest problem which the Government had to face. It came my way so fleetingly that my comments on it would be of small value. It will be for the eventual historian to reconstruct the period, placing each subject in due proportion. My aim is to provide him with a few bricks which might otherwise escape notice.

I kept a diary every night, a cryptic affair scribbled in cheap notebooks. Diaries are not to be trusted. Either they are written for effect, or else they are a safe deposit where the writer stores only those thoughts which he would not express at the time in public. For example, a Minister is constrained to be friendly to his Cabinet colleagues, so he reserves for his diary all the rubs and frustrations which they cause him. Both the friendship and the frustrations are real, and the truth has to include them both. For this reason political diaries make good journalism but bad history. Mine is a check on chronology and a trigger to the memory, no more. Quotations from it are sparse. My only other quotations are from political minutes which I sent to the Prime Minister, usually in manuscript at moments of crisis.

I am deeply grateful to William Waldegrave for his careful reading of the manuscript and for his criticisms. He will see that I have accepted most of them. Any errors or misjudgements which remain are mine.

This book is not written as a defence of the Prime Minister whom I served, nor of his colleagues. I have not glossed over the misjudgements which I saw then, or recognize now. I believe that Mr Heath was a most remarkable patriot and Prime Minister.[1] I also believe that the last months of his premiership were a turning point in British politics, which he almost alone recognized at the time. I will try to substantiate these opinions later on. I do not believe they have clouded my memory and I hope they have not prejudiced my judgement.

[1] It is impossible to write a book of this kind without referring to everyone in the past tense. I apologize to all those lively and energetic people who are thus consigned to history.

CHAPTER ONE

TOWARDS POWER

The house of the British Ambassador in Bonn, though agreeably placed on the right bank of the Rhine, has an important disadvantage for the unwary guest. Each tug, forcing a passage against the current for its string of barges, sends the noise of its struggle through the night into the bedrooms which give on to the river. It was difficult to sleep in the Red Room on the night of 8 May 1970. I got up early and rang Richard Webster, the Director of Organization at Conservative Central Office, to learn the latest political news at home. 'We have lost a good many more boroughs than we expected, and a June election is now perhaps probable. So all this casts a gloom.'[1]

Indeed it was an unsettling day. Mr Heath, Leader of the Opposition, continued his long-planned visit to Bonn, for there was nothing to be gained from cutting it short. He saw Chancellor Brandt and then went to lunch with the German Christian Democrat leaders who had just lost power. They talked avidly about how, through some skilful manoeuvre, they might be back in office in a few weeks. They complained of the sadness of life in opposition. 'Yes,' said Mr Heath, 'and you will find that the first ten years are the worst.' It was that sort of day.

The British Conservatives had by then been in opposition for just over five years. Our fortunes seemed to be plunging badly. Two years earlier we had won by-elections at Meriden, Acton and Dudley with swings averaging over 18% in our favour. As late as December 1969 we had still been doing well. There had been fluctuations since then, but it was fairly clear from the polls and from local election results in the spring that the huge lead which we had accumulated was gone. All was to be done again. On 12 May a Gallup poll showed Labour actually $7\frac{1}{2}$ points ahead which I noted as 'almost incredibly bad . . . A cheerful chattering among Labour men in the corridor.' It was a treacherous foundation for an election campaign.

[1] Unattributed quotations are from the diary already mentioned.

In their admirable book on the 1970 election[1] David Butler and Michael Pinto-Duschinsky warn against the use of military metaphors in writing about general elections. But they warn in vain. Election campaigners themselves are divided between those who talk of a battle and those who talk of a horse race. Each metaphor has its snags, but also its rich images, and we should be lost without them. In the spring of 1970 the Conservative Party was a powerful army which had stood too long in its lines waiting for battle. It had the resources, the organization and the battle plan. It was equipped with policies more elaborate and better researched than any Opposition had ever attempted. Trouble within the ranks had been at least brought under control. The authority of its leader had been painfully established. This Conservative army waited anxiously on the hillside, watching its enemy gather strength in the valley below. This is of course where the metaphor breaks down. For it was the opposing general, the Prime Minister, Harold Wilson, who alone had the power to call an election and set the armies in motion. This he did finally on 18 May, after several days in which no other choice had seemed possible.

The first few days after our return from Bonn were remarkably inactive. The Prime Minister had not yet announced an election date. There was no more planning to be done, yet it was too early to put plans into effect. 11 May, for example: 'A wet day of sane and decent men endlessly taking their own political temperatures, discussing everything, doing nothing.' Three days later Mr Heath flew to Scotland for the annual conference at Perth of the Scottish Conservative Party.

In any political career there are certain shrines which become familiar. Not all are agreeable. I would not choose to spend a private holiday in the conference hotels at either Blackpool or Brighton. The Station Hotel at Perth is by contrast a place of dignified pleasure, spacious, orderly, well-run. I could find my way blindfold to the little room on a half-landing between the ground and first floors where Michael Wolff[2] and I used to set up office for Mr Heath, both as Leader of the Opposition and Prime Minister. Year after year in mid-May we were poised just above the bustle of the hotel lobby, but within easy reach of the digni-

---

[1] *The British General Election of 1970*. Macmillan, 1971.

[2] Michael Wolff, who died in 1976, helped Mr Heath for many years as speechwriter, wise adviser and friend.

taries who might wish to bring us news or views. In Scotland these dignitaries are known as 'office-bearers', a phrase which wherever used immediately reminds me of the Station Hotel at Perth. For there is a sense of ritual about Scottish Party Conferences and a preoccupation with protocol which make them both more exasperating and more fun than their English counterparts.

A Conservative audience in the City Hall at Perth is, however, hard to rouse, and Mr Heath was not a speaker skilled in jerking cool listeners into enthusiasm. He managed it however on 16 May. This may have been partly because they had not realized the sour turn in our apparent fortunes, as measured in the polls and local election results. 'Bad news travels slowly, and they are not yet depressed.' Whether the Scots were ahead of or behind the times, they rallied well to his crisp marching orders. At that time the road back from Perth up the wooded hill into Fife towards Edinburgh was still narrow and twisting. The sun shone through bright spring leaves, and for the first time for many weeks I remember feeling exhilarated. It was not that in reality anything had changed for the better. It was simply that the army had at last struck camp and was on the move.

Attention began to focus once again on its leader. Mr Heath had been elected Leader of the Party in 1965, following the narrow election defeat of 1964 and the resignation of Sir Alec Douglas-Home. Mr Heath was the first Conservative leader actually to be elected. His predecessors had 'emerged' from informal consultations, but this process had been painful, indeed almost suicidal for the Party, after Mr Macmillan's resignation in 1963. Sir Alec sensibly agreed that the rule should be changed. Within months Mr Heath lost the General Election of 1966, but no one at the time held this against him. Most people agreed that he had fought well against a strong popular instinct. The electorate felt that after thirteen years out of office between 1951 and 1964, and eighteen months in office with only a small majority, the Labour Party should be given clear authority to govern.

After 1966 Mr Heath's troubles had multiplied. The lot of a Conservative leader in opposition is rarely happy. The Conservative Party, like the Labour Party, covers a wide range of opinion. The public is accustomed to argument within the Labour Party, and, provided the noise does not become too deafening, this seems to be accepted. Its own supporters, and probably the public as well, require a much higher standard of unity from the Conservative Party. In government a Prime Minister can usually insist on unity but in opposition the party's leader is not so well placed. Mr Heath had to keep the Conservatives together over several issues on which his own views were challenged. There were those who disliked the Party's commitment to membership of the European Community, with which Mr Heath's own career had been closely linked. There were those who still resented his abolition of resale price maintenance when he was at the Board of Trade in 1963–4. Some thought the Party should back Mr Ian Smith and white rule in Rhodesia. Others disagreed with Mr Heath's decision to dismiss Mr Enoch Powell from the Shadow Cabinet in the spring of 1968, within hours of his first explosive utterance on immigration. Last and least, there were a few snobs who sneered at Mr Heath's background.

On each of these issues the critics were different, and it would as usual be a mistake to generalize in terms of Left and Right. The fact was that during 1966–70 Mr Heath had to contend with a feeling within some sections of the Party that he saw too many sides to a question, and refused to give the Party the straightforward down-to-earth leadership which they thought they liked.

He mastered these difficulties with great determination. I joined his Private Office in 1968, within weeks of the break with Mr Powell. I had never seen a man drive himself so hard. Above all, he concentrated on getting round the country. No Leader of the Opposition had visited so many places or met so many people. The planning of his tours outside London was almost a full-time occupation. This sustained effort had its reward. By the time of the 1970 election, active Conservative supporters in the country had a clearer understanding of Mr Heath than most MPs or journalists in London. What they saw they liked, and their loyalty lasted well through adversity. They had many stories to show that he was not an easy man. His speeches were uncomfortably full of facts and figures. He did not always bang the drum. But they knew that his determination to change Britain for the better went well beyond the ordinary phrases and promises of political life.

This determination to change Britain was the key to the policy work which Mr Heath had set in hand as early as 1965 under Sir Alec Douglas-Home's leadership. The policy exercise of 1965–70 lies outside the scope of this book. Perhaps it deserves a book of its own.[1] The work was greater in quantity and higher in quality

---

[1] For more detailed accounts see David Butler and Michael Pinto-Duschinsky (op. cit.) and Robert Rhodes-James's *Ambitions and Realities* (Weidenfeld and Nicolson, 1972).

than any which a political party had previously attempted in opposition. There had been a sustained attempt to go beyond the coining of phrases and striking of attitudes, and to probe the real causes of Britain's poor performance. At a week-end meeting of the Shadow Cabinet and its advisers at the Selsdon Park Hotel in January 1970, most of the loose ends were tidied up, and the priorities established. Today most politicians are more sceptical of grand programmes of betterment than they were in 1970. We have been chastened by experience. For example we are more interested in rates of tax than in schemes of tax reform. Having reformed almost every major institution in Britain except itself, Parliament is not too happy with the results. It is right that we should be more cautious about our own profession, provided that we do not lose faith in it altogether.

In the different, more confident atmosphere of 1970, the way was clear in Mr Heath's mind for a reforming Conservative Government. This Government should resolve to do in the 1970s what Peel had tried to do in the 1840s and Pitt in the 1780s. Those great Prime Ministers had shown that the aim of Conservative reform was not to enlarge the power of the state. It was to sweep away what was antiquated and inefficient in our public institutions, and create a new framework within which the individual could take his own responsibilities and create his own prosperity.

New policies were not enough. The style and method of government also had to be changed. Mr Heath wrote a personal foreword to the 1970 election manifesto which revealed his own approach to politics more plainly than anything else in the campaign. It is a short angry piece which emerged hot from the years of frustration spent watching and despising Mr Wilson's style of government.

> During the last six years we have suffered not only from bad policies, but from a cheap and trivial style of government.
>
> Decisions have been dictated simply by the desire to catch tomorrow's headlines. The short-term gain has counted for everything: the long-term objective has gone out of the window. Every device has been used to gain immediate publicity, and government by gimmick has become the order of the day. Decisions lightly entered into have been as lightly abandoned . . .
>
> I am determined therefore that a Conservative Government shall introduce a new style of government: that we shall re-establish our sound and honest British traditions in this field.
>
> I want to see a fresh approach to the taking of decisions. The

Government should seek the best advice and listen carefully to it. It should not rush into decisions, it should use up-to-date techniques for assessing the situation, it should be deliberate and thorough. And in coming to its decisions, it must always recognize that its responsibility is to the people, and all the people, of this country.

What is more, its decision should be aimed at the long term. The easy answer and the quick trick may pay immediate dividends in terms of publicity, but in the end it is the national interest which suffers. We have seen that too often in the recent past.

Finally, once a decision is made, once a policy is established, the Prime Minister and his colleagues should have the courage to stick to it. Nothing has done Britain more harm in the world than the endless backing and filling which we have seen in recent years . . . Courage and intellectual honesty are essential qualities in politics, and in the interest of our country it is high time that we saw them again.

So it will not be enough for a Conservative Government to make a fresh start with new policies. We must create a new way of running our national affairs. This means sweeping away the trivialities and the gimmicks which now dominate the political scene. It means dealing honestly and openly with the House of Commons, with the press and with the public.

The decisions which a Government has to take affect the livelihood and perhaps the lives of millions of our fellow citizens. No one has any business to take part in public life unless he is prepared to take such decisions with the seriousness which they deserve.

This has always seemed to me a key document. Coming from a lesser man it might have been claptrap, but from him it was not. There runs through it a note of genuine puritan protest, which is familiar in British history, sometimes in one party, sometimes in the other. It is the note struck by Pym against the court of Charles I, by Pitt against the Fox-North coalition, by Gladstone against Disraeli, by the Conservatives in 1922 against Lloyd George. It is the outraged assertion of a strict view of what public life is about, after a period in which its rules have been perverted and its atmosphere corrupted. Commentators later reproached Mr Heath for not creating enough peerages, for failing to link arms in the corridors or gossip in the smoking room of the House of Commons, for refusing to flatter his critics. These crimes, if crimes they were, stemmed from his belief that the government of Britain was too serious a matter to be carried forward in the style of Mr Harold Wilson.

The Conservative election campaign of 1970 was planned, like all campaigns, to avoid the mistakes of the immediate past. In

1964 Sir Alec Douglas-Home had been shouted down in the Bull Ring at Birmingham. We novices were often regaled by the veterans with tales of the damage which this had done. In the most recent general election campaign, that of 1966, Mr Heath, as the Party's new leader, had spent a great deal of time and energy on whistle stops round the country, with little evident profit. There was some evidence that there would be violence again in 1970, particularly if the election was held when the universities were up. So the Leader of the Party must be kept at arm's length from violence. Moreover, Geoffrey Tucker, the pugnacious and able Director of Publicity at Central Office, had dinned into all of us his conviction that the election would be won or lost on television.

Out of all these considerations the election plan was concocted. There were to be three main elements in Mr Heath's campaign. Each morning there was to be the press conference at Central Office in London, immediately after the Prime Minister had finished his press conference on the other side of Smith Square. The middle of the day was to be set aside for television and for thought. Our own party political broadcasts had to be composed, and contributions recorded for the current affairs programmes of the BBC and ITV. In the afternoon Mr Heath was to depart to his evening rally outside London, usually in the Dart Herald plane which we had hired for the campaign. To avert violence these rallies were to be for ticket-holders only, and there were to be no questions, except in Mr Heath's own constituency of Bexley, where the asking and answering of questions had become a tradition and an art. The extracts taken by television from these rally speeches were regarded as their most important feature, and for this reason each hall was thoroughly reconnoitred on Geoffrey Tucker's instructions to establish the correct positions for cameras, lights and microphones.

It is no criticism of the plan to say that it had to be changed. Indeed it would be a criticism of those who ran the election if they had failed to change it. The main structure was not altered. The press conferences continued to dominate the morning, though because of the activities of Mr Enoch Powell they were, until the last week, uneasy and defensive. The briefings upstairs in Central Office before each press conference were my particular despair. Because they were the first event of the day they set the tone for everything which followed. They were held in a tiny room on the first floor at 32 Smith Square into which too many people pushed and jostled with their particular titbit for the Leader. No one had the authority to slam the door in the face of dignitaries of the Shadow Cabinet or of the Party. In the end we provided a half-bottle of champagne each morning so that Mr Heath had at least some antidote to this flow of well-meant advice before he faced the press downstairs.

The campaign plane was also a mistake. It is not as a matter of fact sensible in any circumstances to fly from London to Norwich or Southampton or Cardiff. I do not think we would have ventured on these follies had it not been for Mr Heath's distaste for trains which was evident then, but seems more recently to have been overcome. The twentieth century took its revenge. On 8 June we sat miserable in fierce sunshine on the tarmac at Heathrow while the pilot waited in vain for the appearance from the airline's catering department of the packed lunches, on which we and all the accompanying journalists had relied. Those cross, hot and hungry moments were a low point of the campaign. Mr Heath had however already developed the right response to administrative disasters. Although by nature quick-tempered, he through the years always remained calm whenever through the folly of some private secretary a train was about to be missed, a driver lost the way, or a red box was temporarily mislaid. By lashing out on such occasions he would only have flustered his staff without doing any good, so he kept quiet, or talked of other things. This always came as a relief – and a bit of a surprise.

It was unnerving to travel through this campaign in the company of highly intelligent journalists who were convinced that we had already lost. They were polite, even sympathetic, but they knew the answer, and it was not ours. Two of them were already writing a book during the campaign to explain *how* we had lost. Their starting point was the evidence of the opinion polls, and they sought diligently for incidents and anecdotes to reinforce that evidence, discarding other information which pointed to the direction in which they were not looking.

Perhaps it is now fair to tell the saga of the Newport Pagnell cafeteria, which made a lasting impression on me (later purged by writing a novel, called *Truth Game*). On 4 June Mr Heath spoke at Birmingham. It was one of the few occasions when the campaign plane was given a day's rest; we travelled up by train and back by car down the M1. A luxurious bus was provided for the press party which followed Mr Heath's car. We all stopped at the Newport Pagnell cafeteria and ate egg and baked beans. In a corner of the room sat a newly-wed couple celebrating with friends before leaving for their honeymoon. The young bride-groom came over to Mr Heath's table and asked him to join them. The journalists at adjoining tables could not hear Mr Heath's reply, but they could see that he did not leave his seat. Some of those representing the more expensive papers quickly tired of the Newport Pagnell cuisine and retired to the bus. Mr Heath then went over to the wedding table and chatted to the bride and bridegroom and their friends. Luckily some less grand journalists with shorthand pads went over with him and recorded the conver-sation. That did not prevent one paper from reporting loftily in its next issue that Mr Heath had snubbed the couple and refused to go over to their table. This, they said, was typical of the distant, awkward manner which was losing him the election. When I remonstrated with the paper I was quickly thrown on the defen-sive by their affronted pride. It was a trifling incident, but it showed me how even well-qualified journalists can be led astray by preconceptions. It is admittedly a fault which they share with politicians.

The set-piece evening rallies varied in quality. One, at Ports-mouth, was a complete failure. It was a modern hall, seats too comfortable, acoustics too perfect. The best election meetings are in the old Victorian halls, where the human voice resounds richly from Gothic arches or gilded theatre boxes, and oratory is again encouraged to become an art. The meetings at Birmingham and Manchester were the best of the campaign. As fears of violence receded, the local organizers were instructed to relax the ticket-only rule, people were admitted freely at the door, and we began to come across the hecklers who give spice to any mass meeting.

It quickly became clear however that more was needed. The Prime Minister was making few set speeches. He was darting up and down the country by train, often late, always cheerful, chatting to small groups of supporters, making little speeches out of first-floor windows, shaking innumerable hands in the sunshine. The press and television quickly began to paint a damaging contrast between this folksy campaign, and Mr Heath's aeroplane and solitary set speeches. Towards the end of the first week an important change was made. Conservative area agents were instructed that when Mr Heath came to their town or city he would walk round a shopping centre or a market place before or after his meeting.

The new tactic worked well with Peggy Fenner in the crowded

Saturday afternoon streets of Chatham on 6 June. It worked even better at Exeter two days later. A Conservative leader rarely sees the rural strongholds of his Party in a general election, because it is in the cities that the outcome will be decided. But the airfield for Exeter lies in the Honiton division of Devon, and when we arrived the ladies of Honiton were ranged in formidable strength outside the perimeter fence, like spectators at Whipsnade Zoo. As Mr Heath shook hands through the wire there was much jumping up and down and cheering, and an aunt by marriage of my wife's shouted: 'Tell him many a good horse has won the Derby at thirty-three to one.' There was a roaring mass of people in the Civic Hall of Exeter and crowds in the streets. Later the same day on the outskirts of Bristol one of the Conservative candidates, David Hunt, lined up a regiment of tiny tots in a thunderstorm, all wearing the slogan 'I trust Ted'. The crowd in the pub at Bristol that night was also cheerful, and for the first time the campaign itself began to provide an antidote to the bad news from the polls and the journalists. This new pattern was continued, and the walkabouts were a distinct success. The best were a stroll through Princes Street Gardens in Edinburgh, and some lively skirmishing in support of Winston Churchill in the big shopping centre at Stretford. The sceptics were confounded on two points. First, they had failed to understand that compared to 1966 Mr Heath was in 1970 a well-known figure, whom people liked to see in the streets of their town regardless of their politics. Second, he actively enjoyed electioneering and meeting people, and this showed. The well-worn argument about his lack of the common touch applied to a different part of his life. I quickly learnt that Mr Heath felt far more at home in a crowded street than at a dull lunch party, or a difficult press interview.

Slotted in beside the press conferences and the tours was the all-important television. There is a strong element of luck about current affairs programmes – more luck than bias, I suspect – and in 1970 the luck was on our side. Programmes to which both Party leaders submitted turned out well for us, badly for them. Mr Wilson suffered particularly from a barrage of postcards on BBC *Election Forum* and from Mr Robert Kee's interview on *This Week*. We feared the worst for the parallel interview with Mr Heath, which took place in Glasgow on 10 June. We were late, and there had been far too many people in the car on the afternoon drive from Edinburgh. The studio was in chaos and the ground-rules far from clear. To my surprise the interview was calm and successful.

But, of course, far more than luck is required in television. This is true of current affairs programmes run by the broadcasting authorities. It is even more true of the party political programmes made by the political parties themselves.

There is no doubt that the Conservative programmes in 1970 were a success, and that this was particularly true of Mr Heath's final broadcast. An immense amount of work undertaken by Mr Whitelaw, Sir Michael Fraser[1] and Geoffrey Tucker proved to be worthwhile. Of course this work ranged well beyond Mr Heath himself. But there is one error about Mr Heath and television at this time which needs to be corrected. As often happens, someone (in this case, Mr Wilson) invented a point which others still quote as truth. It is said that those who were involved in advising Mr Heath were trying to twist him out of his own nature and to manufacture a false television personality. Exactly the opposite is true. The experts observed correctly that Mr Heath had two voices – a public voice used for speeches and a private voice used in conversation. The two voices sounded quite different, and the private voice more attractive. Moreover, the private voice used shorter simpler words, whereas the public voice often strayed into jargon. The whole thrust of the expert advice given to Mr Heath (not by me but by others) was that he should use his own private voice and vocabulary, in short that he should be himself.

That advice had to be constantly repeated, and opportunities for repeating it became fewer after 1970. Under pressure of time and in the atmosphere of government between 1970 and 1974 the private voice faded and the jargon returned. After 1974 we began to hear again, as we did in 1970, the genuine accents of a man who believed that political communication was more than propaganda.

[1] Now Lord Fraser of Kilmorack.

CHAPTER TWO

A CLOSE-RUN THING

So much for the mechanics of the campaign. But press conferences, rallies and broadcasts are simply vehicles for carrying messages to the electorate, and leaving impressions behind you which will last until polling day. There is no doubt about the main problem of fighting a general election in this country, or indeed in any democracy. It is the problem of conveying forceful messages simultaneously at different levels. The speech which will satisfy the Editor of the *Daily Telegraph* may drive the Editor of the *Sun* up the wall. The broadcast tailored to the don and his family in North Oxford may be useless for the Cowley car-worker and his family a few miles away. Nor is this simply a matter of style and vocabulary; issues which interest the one may have no meaning for the other. A political party has to campaign right across the front, but it also has to know on which important issues its opponent's standing with the electorate is weakest, and its own policies most attractive. It must then repeat, repeat, repeat. When a politician becomes bored with repeating his election speech he should pause and consider. It may be a bad speech; or he may be on the verge of getting his message across.

We knew that rising prices, and in particular food prices, were the main issues which worried the electorate in 1970. Repeated research proved this beyond reasonable doubt. This then would have to be the 'shopping-basket election'. In speech after speech, broadcast after broadcast, the leaders of the Conservative Party would illustrate the upward surge in prices and the connection between rising prices and Labour's record of high taxation and devaluation.

The Conservative programme for dealing with inflation and the other ills of the nation was set out in the manifesto 'A Better Tomorrow'. This document also summarized the policy work done by the Party in Opposition between 1965 and 1970.

On re-reading, the main text of 'A Better Tomorrow' does not do justice to the themes which it contains. This is partly a matter of style. In his books Lord Beaverbrook wrote a lean, excellent English, but in his newspapers he encouraged a staccato pseudo-dramatic style which manifesto-writers found it easy to imitate. 'A Better Tomorrow' has too many rhetorical questions, and too many sentences without verbs. The abrupt style led to errors of judgement which caused trouble later.

'We utterly reject the philosophy of compulsory wage control.'

'There will be no further large-scale permanent immigration.'

By the end of 1972 the Conservative Government had resorted to a statutory incomes policy, and had admitted large numbers of British-passport holders expelled from Uganda. I believe that these were right and necessary decisions. The mistake was to be so absolute two years earlier in opposition to them.

In spite of the defects in its final form, the 1970 programme is still impressive in its range and self-confidence. It did not, for example, evade those parts of the new policy, namely value added tax, the agricultural levies, and the recasting of housing subsidies, which were likely to be unpopular, but which were essential if the sums were to add up.

The trouble with the Conservative campaign message was that it was not getting through. On Sunday 31 May at the outset of the formal campaign, I wrote: 'We now have an even chance, though HW has tricks in his locker, and we have none.' On Saturday 6 June after a week of campaigning: 'Polls bad again, and a general edgy weariness all round.' The next day was a Sunday, set aside for stock-taking and refreshment. Mr Heath's flat in the Albany Chambers off Piccadilly had a large and pleasant drawing-room where the great men of the Party gathered that morning for coffee. Alongside was the small study where Michael Wolff and I pored over drafts and urgent letters. As far as I can remember there was no serious suggestion from anyone that the course of the campaign should be changed. The next week, the last full week of the campaign, was worse still. Campaign reports from the constituencies were good, everything else was bad. The opinion polls were hypnotic. On the evening of 12 June after Mr Heath's speech at Manchester, I was standing at the back of the Free Trade Hall watching the crowds jostle their way out when a Party official told me that the *Daily Mail* next morning would carry an NOP poll showing us 12.4 points behind. It was the worst yet. There were only six days to go. I went to warn Mr Heath, but he had already left for the hotel. I hurried after him, but was too late. On his way up the stairs from the public lounge to his room a journalist gave him the news and asked for his reaction. I cannot remember his reply, but I can remember the blank look on his face.

This was the week in which Mr Enoch Powell put forward his full strength. None of us doubted the hold which Mr Powell then had over the media and over the popular imagination as a result of his attitude on immigration in 1968.

Mr Powell was standing again as the official Conservative candidate in Wolverhampton South-West, and in his final speech he urged the country to vote Conservative. But in his previous speeches in the campaign he concentrated on immigration and spoke darkly of 'the enemy within'. The impression was of a solitary prophet, filled with scorn for his former friends and colleagues, waiting for the nation to turn to its real leader. Despite recent academic studies it is impossible to judge what effect Mr Powell had on the outcome of the election. It would be impertinent to enquire into his motives. What is certain is that he thoroughly disrupted the campaign of his own party. In particular, Mr Heath's press conferences that week were dominated by questions about Mr Powell. Late in the evening of the Manchester meeting and the terrible opinion poll, we saw the advance text of Mr Powell's speech the next day. He seemed determined that we should lose, and lose badly. It was a dramatic and unsettling moment. I slept at the Travellers Club that night because it was too late to go back to my home in Roehampton. I got up at 6.30 next morning, sat in the splendid library, then still white and red, and composed a powerful piece to rebut Mr Powell, the cleaning ladies bustling around me. The piece was never used, but it eased my mind.

The last Sunday of the campaign provided the chance for a final stock-taking. This time there was a meeting of colleagues at Mr Barber's house in Montpelier Square. The Conservative Party owed a great deal in those weeks to the good sense of its Chairman. Mr Barber was campaigning hard himself in the constituencies, but his cheerful steadiness also helped to prevent backbiting or panic at Central Office. His Deputy, Sir Michael Fraser, used his long experience of general elections to the same effect. I do not know how many of those drinking coffee in the sunny upstairs drawing-room in Montpelier Square on Sunday 14 June expected their party to win the election. If they despaired they were too professional to show it. It was too late to change the content of the campaign, and no one suggested that we should. The discussion was almost entirely on the best way of coping with the challenge from Mr Powell. The colleagues agreed on a short, mild and statesmanlike pronouncement, and issued it at once. They then dispersed and Mr Heath went off to record his last television broadcast.

On Monday 15 June the atmosphere began to lift. At his morning press conference Mr Heath finally threw off the incubus of Mr Powell by saying that he would take no more questions on the subject. He set off in a Land-Rover to tour the London suburbs. In the crowded constituency office at Putney we handed him the unexpectedly bad trade figures in time for him to use them for the rest of the afternoon. There seemed then just a fleeting chance of success.

On Tuesday morning, 16 June, the polls were still bad. That morning Central Office released a background paper on our economic policy drafted by Mr Brian Reading of the Conservative Research Department. Brian Reading was not alone in feeling that, so far as informed opinion was concerned, there was a gap between our concentration on the prices issue and the long-term reforms proposed in the manifesto. As a professional economist he wanted to pull together into a coherent whole what had been said about the way in which we would tackle inflation, so that the economics correspondents of the quality newspapers would realize that we had at least thought the thing through. This was a limited exercise, and his draft hung around for several days waiting for the approval of busy men. At last we thrust it once more before Mr Heath and Mr Iain Macleod, the Shadow Chancellor; it was approved by them and issued in Mr Heath's name. Weeks after the election this paper was made famous by Mr Harold Wilson because of the phrase in it about reducing the rise in prices 'at a stroke'. It joined the large collection of speeches and documents in British political history (including Mr Wilson's own broadcast about 'the pound in your pocket') which are remembered only because opponents have torn a phrase out of context and misused it. At the time Mr Wilson reacted to quite a different part of the document. That Tuesday evening he stood in a field somewhere in Lancashire and denounced the passage in which Brian Reading had argued that Labour policies if continued would lead to another devaluation of the pound. By this miscalculation, Mr Wilson gave Brian Reading's paper unexpected publicity and helped to undermine his own professions that the economy was under control.

By this time Mr Heath and his party were in Bradford for the last big speech of the campaign. Everyone was tired. There was a row at the Yorkshire TV studio over some trifle. The stewards at the rally excluded, because he did not have a ticket, a leading member of the Pakistani community, who later had to be invited and placated at great length by Mr Heath in his hotel room. Finally we got away. There was champagne for everyone on the return trip so that we could say goodbye to the campaign plane in style.[1] It was a great relief to be rid of it.

On Wednesday and Thursday we went to Mr Heath's constituency in Bexley. It was a different world. The opinion polls and the television studios were far away. The seat was by no means safe, and the experienced agent Mr Reg Pye organized matters accordingly. There was an immense army of eager helpers. The King's Head in Bexley High Street was thronged at all legal times with cohorts of Young Conservatives resting briefly from their labours. Those of us who came from London were no longer treated as members of Mr Heath's staff, for there were no more speeches to be drafted, reports to be analysed, or letters answered. We stopped speculating about the outcome. We re-enlisted as raw private soldiers in Mr Pye's army. We canvassed, ran messages, delivered literature. Mr Robert Allan, now Lord Allan, a distinguished former Member of Parliament, had nobly acted as Mr Heath's personal ADC through the campaign, dealing with the inevitable rubs and irritations. He and I were given a special task on polling day. There was a maverick independent candidate in Bexley, who had no known views on any subject, but relied on the fact that having changed his name to E. Heath by deed poll, he appeared as such on the ballot paper. Mr Allan and I were issued with large placards which read: 'To vote for the real Edward Heath, Leader of the Conservative Party, put your X against the BOTTOM name on the ballot paper'. We spent much of polling day patrolling with these in the sunshine outside the polling station at Uplands Primary School. It was a calming and satisfactory occupation.

The count in Bexley took place in the Drill Hall. The Young Conservatives had a radio in an adjoining room. By the time the Bexley result was announced, we had a glimmering of what might have occurred. Because of the way we had spent the last two days, what seemed to matter most was Bexley. When Mr Heath's

---

[1] There is a good deal of champagne in this chapter. I will not repeat the theme, but no account of the 1970 campaign or of Mr Heath's premiership would be complete without it. In fact champagne is the right drink for politics. It stimulates at the time, and does not deaden afterwards. In the nineteenth century it was prized for its medicinal qualities. It is a pity that most twentieth-century politicians have abandoned champagne in favour of other drinks which are heavier and just as expensive.

majority of 8000 was announced we realized for the first time what was afoot. There was cheerful pandemonium afterwards at the tiny constituency office at Crook Log. It was clearly right to return to London at once. The car radio persisted in telling us extraordinary good news. The Conservatives were winning the election handsomely. Extraordinary news to me, but not to Mr Heath. To him it was simply the logical result of the long years of preparation, and of the fact that the people of Britain, like the people of Bexley, were at bottom a sensible lot.

There was a large crowd in Smith Square outside Conservative Central Office, through which Mr Heath had to thrust his way without police protection. One disappointed citizen stubbed out a lighted cigarette on his neck, burning him painfully. It was now well past midnight. Central Office was full of Party workers and of others in dinner jackets. It was not possible to distinguish clearly between those who had borne the heat and burden of the day and those who had come into the vineyard only during the last triumphant hour. It was a relief to go to Mr Heath's flat at Albany, and talk briefly about the morrow. At 4.30 a.m. it was nearly light, and I finally reached home.

No one will ever be sure how the victory occurred. Was it always there under the surface? Or did it come into being in the last three days? The pollsters and all those who had predicted our defeat the week before were of course persuaded that there had been a late swing. The evidence of the polls bore them out, particularly of the ORC poll which continued research later than the others and alone foretold the right result. It could be argued that the bad trade figures, or Mr Powell's final endorsement, or Mr Heath's shrugging off of Mr Powell, or even Germany's defeat of England in the World Cup had helped to persuade people at the last moment to support the Conservatives. None of this is quite convincing. I suspect that the victory was there all the time, and that the margin of error in the polls was wide because people did not want to appear to the pollsters to be backing what looked like a loser. So the press influenced the polls, and the polls influenced the press; each error fed the other. Under the surface people were making up their minds on their impression of Mr Wilson's Government over five years. That impression was sufficiently bad, and the Conservatives sufficiently credible, to sway the balance.[1]

[1] Any serious student of the case against the late swing theory must take into account Mr Rhodes-James's argument about canvass returns in *Ambitions and*

At moments of exhaustion one's emotions are odd. Certainly that night I felt glad for the Conservative Party and for Mr Heath, but little sense of triumph against the Labour Party. My strongest feeling was satisfaction that the experts, the know-alls, and the trend-setters had been confounded.

Realities (op. cit.). Canvass returns are unscientific, but they cover far larger numbers of people than opinion polls. Some are thorough, some not. The Banbury returns quoted by Mr Rhodes-James showed a big swing to the Conservatives throughout the campaign with little variation at the end. Having taken over part of the Banbury seat in 1974, I happen to know that its canvass returns are pretty reliable.

CHAPTER THREE

THE NEW STYLE

In a general election those at the centre have little time to think of themselves. The same must be true in battle. It does not matter whether the campaign is going well or badly, the hubbub and confusion are still compelling. The struggle to fit the necessary events into short days fills the mind and squeezes out thoughts of the future. I had never seriously considered what my position would be if Mr Heath won the General Election of 1970. I vaguely supposed that I would continue to work for him, but we had never discussed it. It would have tempted Providence to raise the subject with him during the election campaign, most of all in the last ten days when as a precaution we had to steel ourselves for defeat. So when he told me on the afternoon of 19 June to go to Ten Downing Street I had to ask how I should announce myself.

'It's perfectly simple. Tell them you are my Political Secretary,' he said, as if reminding me of some obvious fact which I had forgotten.

The only remaining difficulty was that I had no idea what a Political Secretary was or what he did. Nor was there anyone I could ask. There was John Wyndham[1] of course, who had worked unpaid for Harold Macmillan, more as a friend than an employee; but the scene had changed out of recognition since his day. While serving at the Foreign Office I had several times trudged across the gravel of the Horse Guards to the stately rooms in Admiralty House from which Harold Macmillan had directed the Government while Number Ten was being refurbished. His entourage had always been most kind, but also formidable, conducting a mass of business with a casual but deceptive air of amateurism. That reign had ended only seven years before, but it seemed like seventy.

Nor could I ask my immediate predecessor, Mrs Marcia Williams, who was busy packing innumerable files in the attic

[1] Later Lord Egremont.

of Number Ten when I knocked at the door.[1] There is no provision in our system for the victors at any level to consult the vanquished before taking over their responsibilities. In any case, the one point clear to me about my new duties was that I was expected to carry them out in quite a different way to Mrs Williams. At our listening post in Opposition we had heard muffled echoes of the great battles which she had fought for the Prime Minister's soul. At Downing Street I never heard a full account of those battles, though there were many still there who carried scars. There is a pleasant convention in the public service that civil servants do not gossip to politicians of one party about their experiences with the other. This convention runs parallel with the rule that incoming Ministers cannot see the papers of their predecessors. The civil servants would have been embarrassed if I had asked them for the full saga, though over three and a half years I could not help fitting together part of the story anecdote by anecdote. In 1972 Mrs Williams published her fascinating and underrated book *Inside Number Ten*. Though the style is not that of Trollope, there is a strong whiff of Barchester about this work. It is as if Mrs Proudie had set down every detail of her battles with Archdeacon Grantley, Mr Slope and all the others who sought to influence her Bishop without her leave. No issue was too great or too small for Lady Falkender's attention. She fought about the accommodation of her Political Office. She fought about the use of the Prime Minister's time, and captured 'political hours' in the afternoon when he worked under her eye at the House of Commons away from the baleful influence of the civil service. She fought about the handling of correspondence. She fought endlessly about the invitation lists for the Prime Minister's parties. She even fought against the secretaries in the famous Garden Room, whose disastrous social origins were betrayed by occasional twin sets and pearls. She fought fiercely and fatally about the award of honours. And at the end she did not see the connection between this endless in-fighting and the unpopularity of which she was clearly conscious.

But it would be wrong to dismiss Lady Falkender's actions as the fruit of trivial resentments or social envy. On the contrary,

[1] Now Lady Falkender. She caught us on the hop that day because she was understandably anxious to get out of Number Ten at once, but could not do so without taking possession of the Leader of the Opposition's rooms in the House of Commons, which we had made no plans to evacuate. We had refused to tempt Providence.

what she did flowed from a considered analysis of the relationship between Labour politicians and civil servants, which deserves careful study. She argues in her book, rather on the lines of the late Mr Richard Crossman, that civil servants try instinctively to tame and then dominate their Ministers. She holds that Labour Ministers are at a particular disadvantage, because civil servants are Conservative in their instincts. She has a vision of senior civil servants lunching almost daily at clubs in Pall Mall from which she is excluded, if not as a Socialist then certainly as a woman. An incoming Labour Government, pledged to sweeping reform, in her view collides with a civil service which at the senior level is bound by its social background and its political convictions to offer strong resistance. It was her duty to help to make the Prime Minister an irresistible force, and to prevent the civil service from entrenching itself as an immovable object. She does not claim total success in either task, but the struggle was certainly heroic.

My own experience at Number Ten led to a different conclusion. I do not believe that in any important respect the civil service is a natural ally of the Conservative Party. I did not know the voting habits of the civil servants with whom I worked, though sometimes I could guess. What is certain is that these voting habits were far less important than the tradition of public service in which they were trained. That tradition made them scornful of the political struggle, though often fascinated by it. It was the Ministry rather than the Minister which mattered, the general administration of the country rather than the ambitions of each fleeting group of politicians. Indeed this attitude works in practice to the advantage of Labour Governments because allied to it is a firm belief in the merits of action by the state. A Minister who proposes a new form of government activity will find himself promptly served. He will quickly discover in his red box the requisite scheme for a new Board, a new Bill for Parliament, a new network of government offices in each town and city. The Minister who wishes to dismantle part of the machinery of the state has a much harder task, as Conservative Ministers found in 1970-1.

It would be beyond the scope of this book to describe the new system of Programme Analysis and Review which the Heath Government introduced. This was a sophisticated attempt to question from the inside the scope of modern government. Across-the-board spending cuts at moments of crisis were familiar enough – and were to become familiar again. But they were haphazard. They hit the good programmes with the bad. It should surely be possible to look quietly and systematically at the work of each department, and to eliminate those activities which happened because they happened and for no other reason. A system was therefore devised to subject the continuing activities of government to the same searching scrutiny which, in theory at least, is given to proposals for new action. But in practice it was found that each examination of this kind lasted for many months. The arguments against abandoning any particular programme were fiercely sustained by people who, by virtue of their position, knew more of the details than their critics. The truth is that a party which believes in reducing the power of the state will always face serious problems with civil servants at all levels, regardless of how the latter vote, or where they take lunch. Lady Falkender should have counted her blessings.

Mr Joe Haines's book *The Politics of Power* covers much of the same ground as Lady Falkender's. It also suffered much the same fate from reviewers and columnists. The juicy chapters, describing the bizarre wrangles among Mr Wilson's staff, were squeezed to the last drop. The sober chapters went almost unnoticed. But Mr Haines's chapter on the civil service, 'The Master Servants', will have a place in any serious study of British politics. His analysis is more subtle than Lady Falkender's. He does not see Tories lurking behind every civil service desk. He sees the civil servants bemused and disillusioned by the destructive partisanship of political life. No sooner do they work out a policy at the behest of one Cabinet than it is destroyed by another. So in reaction they work out a central line of policy which is their own. Though often compelled to deviate from this central line, they always try to return to it, using tactics which are sometimes far from straightforward. This central line includes incomes policy. It also includes a high priority for the salaries and perquisites of the civil service.

There is some truth in this analysis, but not the whole truth. It is true that civil servants, like most sensible people, regret the way in which the widening gulf between the political parties in Britain has led to bad government. They look wistfully at Germany and the United States where the electorate has a valid choice between political parties without each change of government meaning a total upheaval of policy. It is also true that many civil servants have a liking for incomes policy, just as they like any policy which relies for success on the ingenuity of the state machine. But beyond this it is hard to detect a clear central line to which the civil service hews. On the contrary, the training and instincts of the higher civil servant mean that he needs political direction. It is the fuel on which he operates. Without political direction he stutters, then stops. To change the metaphor, civil servants may sometimes be seen giving artificial respiration to their Minister. It is a violent process, and the outside observer can be forgiven for thinking that they are trying to bully him into something. But in fact they are trying to rouse him so that he can again give them the direction which they need. There are all kinds of defects to the system. The workload of a senior Minister is unnecessarily great. He may forget or be unable to give his department the right leadership. The paperwork multiplies beyond reason. Junior Ministers, who should help the senior Minister run the Department, are often kept in a separate cocoon of minor engagements and paperwork. These are defects which could be put right. They are not evidence of conspiracy.

Not that all this was plain when I stood on the doorstep of Number Ten about teatime on 19 June 1970. I understood only that I was expected to make peace where Mrs Williams had made war.

From the beginning this was an easy task. I was met in the hall by Sandy Isserlis, who not long before had become the Senior Private Secretary at the death of Michael Halls. He showed me my office on the ground floor next to the Cabinet Room, an irregular room with two big windows overlooking the garden and the park beyond – as pleasant a place to work in as I shall find in my life. We talked about the Wilsons' domestic plans, and whether it would be useful to them to be able to live at Chequers for a few days; about handling the flood of letters and telegrams of congratulation which was already pouring in. But the new Prime Minister's first job would be to put together a Government. The jigsaw puzzle was far from complete in Mr Heath's mind, and he and Mr Whitelaw, his Chief Whip, would need to work well into the night. Isserlis made the necessary arrangements for food and drink. The choice of beer and pork pies convinced Willie Whitelaw that much had gone amiss with the standards of public life.

Over the next few weeks the relationship between the Political Office and the civil servants at Number Ten (the Private Office) took its new shape. Several fortresses over which Mrs Williams' tattered flag had flown were abandoned by me. The most important change was the Prime Minister's appointment of a career diplomat, Donald Maitland, to run his Press Office. The whole question of communication from the Prime Minister's office is so crucial that it needs a separate chapter. At the same time we established that the civil servants in the Private Office, not the Political Office, should have the main responsibility for the Prime Minister's diary, for answering letters from MPs, for editing and for drafting official speeches, for the choice of guests at official receptions and for a number of other minor matters. The Political Office, which was much smaller than under Mr Wilson, remained responsible for liaison with the Party and for those parts of the Prime Minister's life, for example his annual visit to the Party Conference, which were mainly party political.

But of course life is too complicated to fit into neat charts of defined responsibility. The political and the official parts of a Prime Minister's job cannot be separated. Nor can his staff, political or official, give him the help he needs unless they work together cheerfully and as friends. This we undoubtedly achieved. Looking back over that time I can see a good many mistakes and remember some arguments. But the overwhelming recollection is of friendliness and good humour – between the Prime Minister and his staff and among all of us who worked for him.

Number Ten Downing Street is a house, not an office, and that is its most important characteristic. In the summer, tourists throng the little street outside. They gape at the policeman and the neat black door. They are polite, but probably most of them go away a little disappointed, convinced that the right adjective for Britain is quaint. Number Ten ranks with Anne Hathaway's cottage and the Bluebell railway line. The Kremlin, the Elysée and the White House by contrast look like real seats of Government. Even when messengers and Ministers come and go through that black door, it is hard to imagine anyone governing anything substantial from Number Ten.

Inside the impression is at first the same. A corridor leads straight from the entrance hall to a small lobby which opens into the Cabinet Room. The Cabinet Room, with the three connecting drawing-rooms and the dining-room on the first floor are the dignified rooms of the house. None of them is magnificent, though all are now handsome. There were hundreds of such rooms in eighteenth-century London. Above the dignified rooms, on the second floor, is a small private flat. Off the dignified rooms on the ground and first floor, and alongside the upstairs flat, are a maze of little offices. Some are pleasant, some are bleak, none is magni-

ficent. The Press Office, the Private Office, the Political Office, the
Parliamentary Private Secretary, the Honours Section, the Garden
Room for the secretaries, the Correspondence Section – all have to
be fitted higgledy-piggledy into two modest town houses back to
back. The mixture of old and new, big and small, formal and
informal is unique in modern Whitehall. But I imagine that all
government departments had something of the same flavour
before the birth of the civil service and the building of the stately
Victorian palaces in which that civil service is still for the most
part housed.

If I was to do my job as Political Secretary properly, I needed
access to the Prime Minister at almost any time, and full information about what was going on. There was no difficulty about
either. A Prime Minister's official day begins about 10 a.m.
Between 9 and 10 Mr Heath held in effect a levée in the upstairs
flat, during much of which he sat in his dressing-gown surrounded
by a pool of abandoned newspapers. Any of us could march in
at that hour to ask a question, deliver a protest, or simply take the
temperature. He tried to keep lunchtime free whenever he could,
and here again was an opportunity to invade the flat. On Tuesdays
and Thursdays he held a forty-minute briefing immediately before
he went to the House of Commons after lunch to answer Prime
Minister's Questions. This institution is often criticized, and from
a parliamentary point of view it lacks substance. But in briefing
himself for his PQs the Prime Minister has a marvellous opportunity to poke his nose into details of the work of government
which would not ordinarily come his way. Departments have to
arm him with facts and figures to deal with any supplementaries
which might arise from the original question on the order paper.
Often these facts and figures would show clearly that a particular
policy was progressing slowly or that some hitherto unreported
danger was emerging. When this happened a brisk telephone call
or minute would be authorized to urge things on. Tim Kitson as
Parliamentary Private Secretary and I as Political Secretary were
there on one of the sofas with the civil servants, so we too had a
chance to chip in. These briefing sessions were fun in themselves
and often more useful as a spur to action than the question time
which followed.

Late in the evening, as the official engagements petered out,
the Prime Minister would often appear in my office to pass the
time of day. 'Well, what's going wrong now?' was his usual style
of greeting. He would riffle through the papers accumulating in

the open black box which I kept on a chair by the side of my desk. The black box was my lifeline. Each night before I left I locked it and took it upstairs to the Prime Minister's flat, having filled it with letters to be signed and whatever political documents I wanted him to see. Next morning a messenger brought the black box back to me. Usually the work had been done, but every now and then when the pressure was intense I unlocked the box and found the contents virgin – letters unsigned, documents unread. Then I would go across the corridor to complain to the Private Secretaries, usually to find that their red boxes had been similarly spurned. There was a friendly competition between my little black box and their multitude of red ones. I used to spice mine with little bits of gossip to tempt the Prime Minister to deal with it first. It also had a great advantage in that it contained the *Morning Cloud* folder with the latest reports or requests for decisions on his boat. On the whole I think the Political Office won the battle of the boxes. Black prevailed over red. Certainly I could never reasonably complain of lack of access to the Prime Minister.

Access was one essential, information was another. It was no good going to see the Prime Minister about some great matter unless before entering the room you knew the state of play. He could not be asked to act as an information bureau. You were expected to have read the documents, to know the different points of view before you offered your own. I had no right to go to meetings of the Cabinet or of Cabinet Committees; but there were often informal meetings of Ministers with or without officials where I could sit discreetly on a windowseat, fairly sure that no one would think it worth the trouble to turn me out.

It was also an advantage to have my office next to the Cabinet Room. This was a boon which I owed to Lady Falkender. Geography in these matters is certainly next to godliness. Ministers waiting for Cabinet to begin, Ministers emerging glum or triumphant after it was over, even one Minister (Tony Barber) coming out for the quick cigarette he was forbidden inside – for these the Political Secretary's room was for a few minutes a haven for easy chat.

My security clearance meant that I could see classified papers. The difficulty was to know what I needed to see in order to keep abreast of those parts of the work of government which were politically important. It took some time to find the right answer. Tea was taken in common in the junior of the two Private Office rooms. Clutching my cup and saucer I used to wander into the senior room where along one wall stood the different trays filling with the papers which would go into the red boxes that night – labelled Action Immediate, Action, Foreign Office telegrams, and so forth. By skimming through these papers I could get in less than half an hour a fairly clear idea of what was going on. Robert Armstrong, who had taken over from Isserlis as the Senior Private Secretary a few months after the 1970 election, also let me look through his pending tray, which usually held the minutes of the latest Cabinet and Cabinet Committee meetings. These arrangements would never have been possible if everyone had stood on their constitutional rights. I was probably helped by the fact that I had been a government servant myself for fourteen years, so that I spoke the language. But overwhelmingly this easy co-operation came about because of the understanding attitude of the civil service private secretaries, and in particular of Robert Armstrong.[1] They understood my needs and did their best in many ways to meet them. They accepted that there was a political dimension to the Prime Minister's life and that this could not be strictly defined. They expected in return only that I would not complicate their lives unnecessarily. With different individuals and in more difficult circumstances we re-created the easy informality of Harold Macmillan's Private Office. This is the only spirit in which Number Ten can be run.

Nevertheless, looking back, I feel dissatisfied; not with the co-operation just described, which was certainly right, but with the quantity and quality of political help which the Prime Minister actually received. Political advice and civil service advice need to be properly balanced in a Prime Minister's diet. Yet in our system civil service advice is preponderant, and political advice is crowded out by the sheer pressure of events. But what is political advice? It is not simply saying 'Prime Minister, the 1922 Committee won't like this' or 'Remember next Thursday is the Hove by-election'. Nor is it weighing policies in terms of votes at the next general election. There is nothing disreputable about any of these kinds of advice, for politics is about persuasion. Votes are the easiest available measurement of political efficiency, just as profits are the easiest available measurement of business efficiency. Both are crude but necessary tests. It is admittedly often a mistake for the politician to rush for the immediate electoral advantage, as it is for the businessman to build up immediate profits by running down his assets. Nonetheless, the criticism that

[1] Now Permanent Secretary at the Home Office.

a politician is seeking votes is not a criticism, since without votes he is as useless to the community as a businessman who makes no profits.

But political advice goes wider than this. The political adviser must try to relate the immediate problem to the general mood and state of the nation. He watches the strategy of the Government to see how its policies knit together and what impression they are creating. He watches the personalities of the Government for signs of strength or exhaustion. He watches the reaction to the television and radio broadcasts, some of which Ministers make but hardly any of which Ministers see or hear. His is an imprecise, unending job. When things go smoothly he need make few demands. But in rough times, when existing policies have collapsed, a Prime Minister will find that the senior civil servants fall silent. I saw this happen once over Ireland and three times over incomes policy. They busy themselves at such times with the usual agendas and meetings, the corridors are full of scurrying figures, but nothing substantial emerges. They are, quite reasonably, waiting for the new course which only politicians can set. It is then that the political advice becomes all-important.

Of course the main and best source of this advice must be a Prime Minister's own Cabinet colleagues. Some of them may be his rivals, but the British system can usually ensure that almost all of them are his friends as well. He needs to listen to as many of them as he can outside the formal meetings of the Cabinet and its Committees. There will be three colleagues, the Leader of the House, the Chief Whip and the Chairman of the Party, on whom a Conservative Prime Minister must particularly rely for political advice at the top level. Unless he respects their judgement and (just as important) enjoys their company, a Government will not run smoothly.

Below that level a Prime Minister chooses how he is to be served with political help in Number Ten. My conclusion is that he needs more powerful help than I could provide in 1970–4. Although I had been a government servant I was one no longer, so had no automatic entry to that world. Although I knew most Ministers and many Members of Parliament quite well I was not a member of either House, and there were doors which naturally stayed closed. I do not favour a big Prime Minister's department, which would probably cause more trouble than it was worth. Maybe Mr Wilson's innovation in 1974, when he installed Bernard Donoghue in Number Ten at the head of a policy unit, is the right answer. In his book Mr Haines describes how this worked, and makes a persuasive case. One possibility would be for a Minister who might be Chancellor of the Duchy of Lancaster working at Number Ten under the Prime Minister. He should be a peer, or some other person in whom political ambition is largely spent by reason of age, position, or unselfish character. He should probably be a member of the Cabinet, but his duty there would be to listen rather than talk. Such a Minister would be the Prime Minister's extra ears and eyes in Whitehall and in the Party. He would listen to those important or self-important people for whom somehow a Prime Minister can never find time. He would have easy access to Ministers and to permanent secretaries. He would monitor the progress of the initiatives which a Prime Minister often takes in Whitehall. He would also supervise the general information effort of the Government.

The job is relatively easy to define. So is that of a saint in heaven. The difficulty lies in finding the right person. He or she would need to be patient, sympathetic, humorous and hard-working. A mixture of Machiavelli and St Francis might do, or of Sir Thomas More and Lord Hankey. The difficulty is tremendous. But the need would, I think, be accepted by most of those who have worked close to the heart of British Government.

The need stretches beyond Ten Downing Street. A Cabinet Minister needs extra helpers as well as the Prime Minister. They may be special advisers whom he brings in from outside because they have professional experience in the field covered by his department. They will keep him in touch with thinking outside Whitehall on his particular subjects. Or they may be political advisers to help with that side of his life. It is easy for a Minister to be swallowed up in the engrossing work of his own department. He can lose touch with colleagues, with his Party, with the political strategy of the Government. If questioned, he will deny this indignantly. 'What nonsense! I see them all the time.' So he does, on formal or purely social occasions, but he has lost real contact, he is drifting out of sight.

Seeing this happen, I tried in 1972 and 1973 with Mr Heath's approval to interest several of his senior colleagues in choosing political or special advisers of their own. Some had them already; for example, Brendon Sewill was at the Treasury, and Miles Hudson at the Foreign Office. Others did not see the point. Others saw the point, but could not find the right person. The choice must be personal. I could suggest names, but only the Minister could say whether the face fitted.

Slowly we made progress. Maurice Macmillan took on Robert Jackson at Employment, Peter Walker took on John Cope at Trade and Industry. William Waldegrave crossed from the Central Policy Review Staff to the Political Office at Number Ten as my eventual successor. As things became desperate, the newcomers began to join the veterans in occasional meetings in my office at Number Ten. It would be absurd to claim that we made much difference, though we would have made more difference if as a team we had come into being earlier.

There is sometimes in outside comment a confusion between political advice and the Central Policy Review Staff, or Think Tank, which Mr Heath established under Lord Rothschild. The CPRS, which serves the Cabinet, not the Prime Minister, is not concerned with party politics. It is, or should be, a powerful task-force drawn from several disciplines, operating at the centre of Whitehall and free from cramping departmental loyalties. In Mr Heath's time it had a varied role. Lord Rothschild roamed like a condottiere through Whitehall, laying an ambush here, there breaching some crumbling fortress which had outlived its usefulness. He wrote in short sharp sentences; he made jokes; he respected persons occasionally but rarely policies. He had the independence of position and personality which was needed to make the CPRS a success from the start. The Cabinet and the Prime Minister began to load politically urgent tasks upon them. They were asked to study energy, Rolls-Royce, Concorde, race relations, and much besides. Because they were few in number these studies began to get in the way of their general job of monitoring the work of Whitehall in the interests of intellectual consistency and common sense. They were not able, for example, to follow up as decisively as some of us hoped the PAR exercises already mentioned above. An innovating Government, particularly a Government which wants to limit the power of the state, will almost certainly need a small central unit like the CPRS, staffed with intelligent, irreverent people, able to provide the grit for the oyster. To take an example which Mr Heath used, there might be a proposal to spend £500 million on some project. Civil servants from the Treasury and the interested departments meet and disagree. At a higher level they meet and disagree again. At length at the highest level of the official machine, a compromise is worked out. The project is sanctioned, but at half the original figure. The first senior Ministers know of it is when they read an agreed official recommendation that £250 million be spent. It is within their spending targets. Busy, anxious to turn to the next subject, relieved that there is no argument, Ministers agree. Before that happens, the CPRS, having monitored the arguments, should have a chance to say: 'There is a case for spending nothing. There is a case for spending £500 million. There is no case at all for spending £250 million. The compromise would give you the worst of both worlds.'

Another task of the CPRS was to organize occasional reviews of government strategy by Cabinet Ministers. These were extraordinary occasions. Ministers would gather upstairs at Chequers round a long table. At one end sat Lord Rothschild, flanked by the more articulate members of his team. Taking subjects in turn, they would expound, with charts and graphs, the likely consequences of government policy. Their analysis was elegant but ruthless. They made no allowances for political pressures. They assumed the highest standards of intellectual consistency. They rubbed Ministers' noses in the future. It is a tribute to Mr Heath that he instituted these reviews, and to his colleagues that they endured them. They were at once abolished by Mr Wilson.

There is no formula in any of these matters. Each Prime Minister will organize the way in which the Government receives advice, and the mode of his or her own life, differently. Some, like Mr Heath, will live in the upstairs flat, because it suits their personal circumstances. Others will not because it doesn't. Some will have a senior friend or colleague whom they will want to bring in; others will prefer a younger, less experienced staff. Prime Ministers should not be held to an established pattern. They should use the informality of Number Ten to introduce whatever pattern puts *them* at ease, enables *them* to perform to their own satisfaction. They will certainly want channels open to the outside world. They will need to keep in close touch with political supporters. They will want a means of checking the information with which departments supply them. They will want to keep up with old friends. They will want time for refreshment and for family life. But in each case the mixture of requirements will be different. Number Ten should never have the rigid structure of a typical government office.

CHAPTER FOUR

ELEGY FOR EMPIRE

Throughout the years covered in this book there was a general notion among otherwise well-informed people that Mr Heath cared a great deal for Europe and nothing for the rest of the world. It is easy to understand how this notion arose. Mr Heath made his name as the Minister who tried to negotiate Britain's entry into the European Community in 1961-3. The greatest and most lasting achievement of his Government was precisely that event ten years later. It would be silly to write a book such as this without choosing Europe as the theme for a chapter. But in the years immediately before the 1970 election, and in the months which immediately followed it, Europe demanded less of his time and attention than Africa and Asia. This was not because dramatic events in those continents forced themselves on his attention. Rather it was a deliberate, though on the whole unsuccessful, effort by Mr Heath to persuade his fellow citizens to bestir themselves. For he believed that by an effort of will Britain could if she wished retain a distinctive role in what he believed to be two vital areas: the Gulf and Singapore-Malaysia. A third area, the Cape, added itself to the other two in 1970, more by accident than forethought. The positions then still held by Britain east and south of Suez were to him not just lingering rays from the sunset of empire. Properly used they could be the start of a new and exciting enterprise.

It would be interesting to study in greater depth the reaction of individual British Conservatives to the abandonment of empire. A few, surprisingly few, actively resisted it. A few hurried it along. The majority, including Winston Churchill and Harold Macmillan, accepted the change with weariness rather than enthusiasm. They successfully clothed it with phrases and gestures which the Conservative Party would accept. Mr Powell trod his own lonely path from strong imperialist to European to deep and gloomy nationalist. Mr Heath, starting from a strong European conviction, was drawn into a belief in Britain's overseas role which was partly reasoned and partly romantic.

After the French veto on our European application in January 1963, Mr Heath had stayed at the Foreign Office as a Cabinet Minister with the title of Lord Privy Seal, a junior partner of the Foreign Secretary Sir Alec Douglas-Home until October of that year. The responsibilities allotted to him already included the Gulf, and he signed the agreement of 1961 bringing to an end Britain's special position in Kuwait. It was from this time that his fascination with the Gulf can be dated. His own background had of course been distinctly unimperial. He lacked any feeling that in dealing with the rulers and peoples of the Gulf he was dealing with inferiors. On the contrary it was the subtle intelligence of the rulers which constituted their main charm. What they needed was a power which could hold the ring in their traditional quarrels, advise them on necessary political and economic progress, and deter any aggression from outside. This was a job which Britain had done with a handful of men for many years with almost total success and a minimum of fuss. The nature of the job would change, but there was no reason why Britain should not continue to do it.

Against the background of this thinking it was natural for Mr Heath to detest and denounce the Labour Government's announcement in 1968 that Britain intended to pull out of the Gulf by the end of 1971, in disregard of Britain's treaties and of recent assurances given to our friends by a Labour Minister. The Gulf at the time was fairly quiet, but it seemed unlikely that it would remain so. Ancient rivalries kept in check by the British presence smouldered and occasionally flared. The Shah of Iran was actively pushing his claim to Bahrain. The war in the mountains of Oman was a continual worry. So was the quarrel between Saudi Arabia and Abu Dhabi over the Buraimi oasis. There was plenty of scope for troublemakers from outside. The obvious answer to the basic disunity of the Gulf was for the rulers to settle their differences and pool sufficient sovereignty to deter their outside enemies. That much was common policy on both sides of the House of Commons. The question was whether the British should continue their protection while this was happening, or whether a firm announcement of British withdrawal by a fixed date (certainly involving a breach of faith) would concentrate the rulers' minds and hustle them perforce into the modern world.

Mr Heath decided to visit the Gulf in March 1969, and took

with him his Parliamentary Private Secretary Tony Kershaw and myself. It was the first of many foreign expeditions undertaken with him in the next five years, and also the most fascinating, except perhaps for the visit to China in 1974. It was clear from the beginning that we were about to strain the normal conventions which govern the attitude of the Foreign Office to overseas forays of the Leader of the Opposition. Usually the conventions work well enough. The Leader of the Opposition is entitled to as much briefing as he needs before he goes. He can expect when abroad to stay at our Embassies if he wishes, and to make use of their facilities. He is in practice usually treated very much like a visiting Minister. The Ambassador would not always go with him for his discussions with foreign dignitaries, but could expect to receive some account of what happened. In return the Leader of the Opposition observes the convention that he does not directly attack Her Majesty's Government while he is abroad.

This sensible relationship must of course come under strain whenever there is a clear disagreement between the parties on policy towards the countries being visited. Foreign Office officials, bred in the tradition of bipartisanship, regard such disagreement as unnatural and wrong. They tend, even more than home civil servants, to attribute disagreement to the ignorance, and perhaps the obstinacy of the Opposition. If only Mr Heath saw a few more telegrams, if only he met a few more experts, then surely he would realize that he was wrong. Officials who until a few months before had warmly defended Britain's presence in the Gulf now bent their efforts to prove that in the eyes of all sensible men it was an anachronism. Contrary to left-wing belief, the spirit of the age is always firmly entrenched in the Foreign Office.

A briefing session at Mr Heath's flat in the Albany on 25 March before we left for the Gulf was a disaster. Mr Heath exploded in the face of Geoffrey Arthur, a senior Foreign Office official with much experience and a reputation for plain speech. The Foreign Office was accused of feebleness and bad faith. We were clearly set for a stormy ride. Moreover the advance planning of the practical arrangements quickly became a nightmare. Even with the help of a plane from British Petroleum for part of the journey it was almost impossible to produce a credible piece of paper showing how in thirteen days we could get to grips with Iran, Kuwait, Bahrain, Oman, all the main Trucial States of the Gulf, Saudi Arabia, Egypt and Israel. Yet somehow we did.

The paper travel plan was destroyed at the outset. We were

sitting in a plane at Heathrow waiting for take off when the Iran
Ambassador bustled aboard to say that the Shah was going
Washington for General Eisenhower's funeral and would thus be
out of his country while we were in it. It was a bad blow, for it had
seemed essential to know the Shah's mind before we set off round
the Gulf. But it was too late to change plans. In Tehran my head
became rapidly congested with spring dust, and I felt low and
inadequate. We were lavishly entertained by the Foreign Minister
Mr Zahedi and despatched for similar treatment in Shiraz and
Isfahan, including a trip by helicopter to Persepolis.

Then we flew to the south coast and Kharg Island, 'formerly
convicts and gazelles, now a vast jetty and tankers and a super-
market and computers and hideousness, plus the Prime Minister,
who turns out unexpectedly and incredibly to have chosen the
island for his holiday home and gives us all buffet lunch, sailors
patrolling the scrub outside'. Mr Hoveyda was cheerful and
friendly, like all the Persians who received us, but there was no
way, in the absence of the Shah, of pinning them down to a clear
view of Britain's role in the Gulf. What was evident was their lack
of regard for the Gulf rulers, and their determination that Iran
should be the dominant military power around her own shores.

Two days in Kuwait followed. The members of the ruling family
were soft in manner, intelligent and sceptical. Conscious that
they ruled a rich, tiny and vulnerable country, they above all
wanted to avoid fuss. They would have liked Britain to stay, but
since she had announced that she was going, only fuss was likely to
result if she again changed her mind.

Mr Heath was at his best during the next crowded week of
interviews with Arab rulers, punctuated by disagreeable meals and
short bumpy rides in a small plane. He was immensely courteous
and patient. He remembered exactly the particular interests,
history and idiosyncrasies of each ruler. He set out his own
position with the right blend of deference and firmness. He
enjoyed the company of these subtle men, and conveyed that
enjoyment to them. It was a better display of diplomacy than any
I remember during fourteen years in the Diplomatic Service. His
moments of brusqueness and impatience were reserved for occasional British officials or businessmen. This was a contrast which
marked almost all our foreign expeditions.

It would be too long a diversion to describe the different
atmosphere of each sheikhdom in which we spent a few hours, but
Muscat and Oman must be an exception. We spent the morning of

3 April on the island of Masirah where Britain had an air base. Mr Heath spent some time looking for flat land where a new runway could be built.

Then we flew to Salalah, the palace of the Sultan of Muscat and Oman. The old Sultan rarely left Salalah except for the Dorchester Hotel in London. He never visited his capital, Muscat, and hardly ever the rest of his kingdom. He ruled with absolute power, and did not like spending, let alone borrowing money. He was thus the despair of all progressive persons.

There was a small RAF airstrip at Salalah, where a ragged guard fired a salute in our honour. Beyond lay the range of barren mountains of Dhofar in which the Sultan's forces under British officers fought their small, fierce, and apparently endless war against rebels financed and armed from South Yemen. We were met by the melancholy Crown Prince, who later drove his father out. He conducted us silently in a Land-Rover to the white inner courtyard of the Palace. The Sultan waited on the steps to greet us, a small round figure, dignified by his great white beard, softened by large eyes with long lashes. The Crown Prince was excluded, and the Sultan lunched alone in our company. He had just bought, from Harrods I think, a large and hideous revolving table with which he was greatly pleased. It was in effect a huge dumb waiter. He could thus eat his meals without the presence of a servant to bring and remove dishes. The menu was not elaborate. There was soup, lamb with rice, and tinned jelly from Australia, with little cubes of tasteless fruit imprisoned in it. A photographer darted in and out taking innumerable snaps.

The Sultan spoke freely and with a twinkle. His English, very soft, was better than and different from that of the Arab rulers of the Gulf proper, for through the quirks of empire he had been educated and trained as an Indian prince.

Things, he said, were going really rather well. There were still rebels in the hills, but the situation was better than it had been. For the first time in his life he had a good income from the growing oil revenues. People were always urging him to spend it. Of course he intended to spend it. There were so many projects he had dreamed of achieving for his people. Now he could begin to do them. But the great thing was not to be in too much of a hurry. The Americans were always urging him to spend money on great hospitals and schools, not at all what his people needed. Even some of his British advisers were giving odd advice nowadays. They did not seem to realize that if you brought change too quickly, much trouble came with it. The Crown Prince? Yes, one day perhaps, some kind of responsibility could be found for him, but meanwhile he was immature. As for himself, he was glad to say that he had never felt younger or more energetic. Visit his capital Muscat? Yes, why not, but of course a step like that would need very careful thought. It was not the sort of decision to be taken in a rush. And so on for a fascinating hour.

One often hears in the West views which can justly be described as reactionary. They are usually produced *pour épater le bourgeois*. There was nothing of that with the Sultan. Out of politeness he made verbal concessions, with a twinkle, to the ideas which he knew were in our heads. But he did not believe in them at all. For me the idea of total and carefully considered conservatism will always be linked with the old Sultan of Muscat and Oman softly conversing while, through the embrasure, the spring wind drove the waves up the beach towards his palace walls.

During the next three days we travelled at breakneck speed up the Gulf to Bahrain, eating and talking with five rulers in their different capitals, arguing with our diplomatic representatives, drinking with businessmen and soldiers. At Sharjah the last licks of paint were being administered to the brand new British military base established by Mr Healey three years earlier, now to be abandoned. Each ruler displayed his individual brand of subtlety, but basically their reaction was the same. The British and their funny ways were of course familiar; but the notion of a Leader of the Opposition telling them of a policy different to that of the British Government was new and puzzling. The policy proffered by Mr Heath was in many ways attractive. He told them that after all the British might stay. Neither they nor their subjects had shown much desire to be rid of the British. It was several years since President Nasser had seriously tried to stir up nationalism in the Gulf. The British presence had enabled them to come to terms with their new oil riches in an atmosphere of calm, marred only by their traditional, almost affectionate disputes with one another. But in 1968 the British Government had announced a firm date for withdrawal. Was it really feasible that another British Government would or could reverse that decision? How would Egypt react? Or Iraq or Russia; or the Shah with his ancient claim on Bahrain and his new military strength? Were they to believe this forceful, knowledgeable man, or was it more prudent to believe the representatives of the British Foreign Office, who were more evidently in tune with the spirit of the age? The rulers were not themselves keen on the spirit of the age, but they felt it was there. Sensing their dilemma, Mr Heath asked for no commitments. He pressed for no firm reaction. He simply said that when elected we would consult our friends, and that if our friends wanted us we would stay. Each conversation ended on a note of vague yet enthusiastic friendship.

The Shah had by now returned from President Eisenhower's funeral, and sent a Fokker Friendship to Dahran on Easter Saturday to pick us up. At Tehran airport in my capacity as baggage master I spent the small hours searching for some missing suitcases. Easter morning was peaceful. While Mr Heath saw the Shah alone, Tony Kershaw and I at the British Embassy admired the almond blossom, the wisteria, and the caricature of Lord Curzon in the lavatory. As can happen when high personages meet alone, there was a dispute afterwards about what had been said. The account of the Shah's attitude which Mr Heath gave us in the plane that afternoon, and which appeared later in more general form in *The Times*, was more forthcoming than the Iranians would accept.

Slightly weary now, we turned homewards. Saudi Arabia, Egypt and Israel, King Feisal, President Nasser and Mrs Meir were hardly dull fare, but to me at least they lacked the drama of the Gulf. We reached home on 11 April, after an expedition of thirteen days which had felt like thirteen weeks.

All the time of course the real problem was here at home. The obstacle to a continuing British presence in the Gulf did not lie with the rulers or their people, or with the Shah. Nor, at this period, was it the result of lack of money. We had simply lost the will to continue the effort, and Mr Heath was unable to revive it. On 25 April, after several days of work on press conferences, newspaper articles and the compiling of records, I wrote in my diary: 'We are isolated from everyone on this, and can only persevere if there is a real change of nerve over the next few years – dubious.' So it proved. By the time Mr Heath became Prime Minister in June 1970, the Foreign Office was able to argue that it was too late to reverse the decision, that the Gulf was still stable, and that the rulers had managed to come together for their own defence more successfully than we had expected. Their advice was not resisted, for events had moved on. As often happens, the old arguments seemed irrelevant.

The other half of the East of Suez argument concerned Singapore. The British presence here was much more substantial, but under Mr Healey's plans it too was to be dismantled by the end of 1971. This again was an area which Mr Heath knew as a result of his time as a Foreign Office Minister. Here too his emotions as well as his intellect persuaded him that it was wrong to pull out completely. As early as August 1968 he had proposed in a speech in Canberra that stability against external threat could be helped by a new Commonwealth force which would include contributions from Britain, Australia, New Zealand, Singapore and Malaysia. At the end of 1969, he decided that he could carry the idea a stage further by going to South East Asia himself, much as he had gone to the Gulf that spring.

Not that the East of Suez argument was the main reason for this expedition. His principal aim was to win the Sydney-Hobart race in *Morning Cloud*. This was a feat of organization and daring in the face of great obstacles which only sailors can appreciate to the full. For the rest of us it was a symbol of something we already knew, that we were dealing with a remarkably determined and resourceful man. For the British public, if not for some members of the Labour Party, it dispelled the idea that Ted Heath's sailing had anything in common with the leisurely cruises of millionaires in pursuit of luxury and the sun. I doubt if Mr Heath has ever cruised in his life.

During the six years that I worked for Mr Heath there were three *Morning Clouds*. I never set foot on any of them. He rightly preferred to keep that side of his life as separate as possible. Anyway once at sea I would certainly have fallen overboard or performed some other folly. It was therefore natural that I should fly out to Australia only after the race was over. It was not easy to disentangle Mr Heath from his crew, for hard celebration after an event is evidently as important a part of sailing as hard training before it. He managed to take a day off from the parties to see the Prime Minister, Mr Gorton, in Canberra, leaving Tony Kershaw and myself in Sydney to deal with a flood of congratulations.

Eventually on 4 January 1970, we left for Djakarta. It was important to win Indonesia's acquiescence in the new Conservative policy. The last time that British military power had been used in South East Asia had been in the middle 1960s against President Sukarno's efforts to swallow up British Borneo and Sarawak, just as they were becoming the Eastern part of the new Malaysia.

Sukarno had gone, but Indonesia remained vital. If his successor President Suharto had reacted strongly against the idea of a five-power Commonwealth force, it would probably have been still-born. His role in this respect was not unlike that of the Shah *vis â vis* the Gulf.

We need not have worried. Djakarta itself, with its desolate half-finished skyscrapers, was a clear warning against Sukarno. President Suharto was heeding the lesson. 'A command post of blue berets, cocks in a cage, inside gay fish darting about a tank, plus two tigers. He [Suharto] reserved and friendly. EH puts across the policy very well . . . Suharto answers understandingly, should be no repetition of Shah incident.'

We spent 6 January in Kuala Lumpur consulting the Malaysians. It was the first time I had set foot in Carcosa, the magnificent house of the British High Commissioner. Of the British palaces in the East which I have seen it is the most attractive, with the exception of the old Legation in Peking, now gone for ever. Poverty may force us out of these palaces, but policy should not. Those, mainly British diplomats, who argue that politically speaking we would be better off without them misunderstand the link between past and present. After all, Indians, Malays and Chinese do know that there was a British Empire and that these are its monuments. Some respect that past, some dislike it; but we will not escape our part in history by camouflaging ourselves in suburban villas, as if we were Swiss or Nicaraguans.

The Malaysians were preoccupied with their communal problem, to which British forces were not relevant, but their history since independence showed them that their security from external threat could not be taken for granted. The British, Australians, and New Zealanders were part of their landscape. A modest Commonwealth force based, not on imperial power, but on willing co-operation was welcome to them. For them the difficulty lay not with the white Commonwealth countries, but with Singapore and its Prime Minister Lee Kuan Yew. The younger Malaysian Ministers were suspicious of Lee's links with their own Chinese politicians, and they resented the good-humoured contempt with which he treated their efforts to solve problems from which Singapore was free.

The Tunku himself, then still Prime Minister of Malaysia, was above such humdrum considerations. We dined with him in Kuala Lumpur in a house tightly packed with objects recalling his past. He availed himself ruthlessly of the privileges of old age. Every attempt to start a serious discussion was diverted into an anecdote and a joke. His Ministers and the English visitors gathered round his table were treated affectionately as children, only slightly more grown-up than his grand-daughter playing with the tiger's head on the floor. We ate sizzling steaks and *crêpes suzette*, and drank wild honey in our coffee.

The next two days in Singapore were more strenuous. There were British officials, businessmen, Service commanders, and journalists, with each of whom a separate session was arranged. But mainly there was the Prime Minister Lee Kuan Yew, a man of the first rank, formidable because he knew England so well. He knew and approved the policy which Mr Heath brought with him, and was prepared to show it by the way he received us. But in return we had to understand what he was about. He gathered his Ministers together and gave us a concentrated briefing on the future of Singapore.

Only the French and the Chinese keep through twists of fortune a firm confidence in their own future. They are too polite to say openly that this confidence comes from the belief that they are superior to the rest of us barbarians, but after a time one can guess. Lee conveyed forcefully his vision of a Singapore which would drive the lazy old ports of the East out of business by ingenuity and hard work, and make itself the commercial capital of South East Asia, essential alike to Japan, Europe and America.

Mr Heath and Mr Lee Kuan Yew had much in common. They were both determined men, who could be hard in their ways. They were patriots. They shared an appetite for facts and for work, and a distaste for the kind of politics represented for them both by Mr Harold Wilson. Yet the two men circled each other warily. Seeing them together several times in the next few years, I tried to work out why this was. I think it happened because they disagreed about the future of Britain. Mr Heath believed that Britain was capable of great things in the future as in the past. This was not platform rhetoric, but his driving force. Lee Kuan Yew thought he knew better. He was willing to give Mr Heath a chance, but he believed the decay had gone too far for one man or one government to put right. The question is still open.

After a visit to Hong Kong we returned to London. The end of a tour of this kind was always the start of frantic days of hard work. Catching up on what had happened at home, dictating records, drafting dozens of thank-you letters, working on speeches and articles – this was the moment when one sighed in Opposition for the resources of Whitehall. It was important that Mr Heath should make quickly a major speech expounding the policy more fully than ever before, and dealing with the main criticisms which had been levelled against it. This he did at the Colston Hall in Bristol on 16 January, before an excellent audience. Old speeches do not warm up well. Enthusiasm for causes which have crumbled cannot easily be revived. I would simply refer to this speech any historian who may be tempted to dismiss the East of Suez policy as just a sop to ill-informed nostalgia, to generals brooding in armchairs. Of course there was some sentiment in it, as there should be in any policy offered to the British people. But there was also a shrewd understanding of what the modern world is about, and of the penalties which attach to a nation which having been great only wants to forget what it once did.

The endless ironies of politics are part of its fascination. The argument about British policy in the Gulf and in Singapore-Malaysia had by 1970 been strongly contested for two years. One might have expected it to continue after a Conservative election victory. It seemed to be established as one of the main issues which divided the two main parties. But instead of continuing it disappeared. Mr Heath's Government withdrew from the Gulf after all, without serious Conservative protest. Lord Carrington as Secretary of State for Defence achieved the proposed five-power arrangement based on Singapore, without serious Labour protest. There *was* a serious and bitter row in 1970 about Britain's overseas role. The Government *was* severely harassed and criticized on foreign policy during its first months of office. But the issue was entirely different and unexpected.

The sale of arms to South Africa had not been an issue at the election of 1970. It was not even mentioned in the Conservative manifesto. The Conservative Opposition had earlier criticized the Labour Government's decision to stop arms sales, and had drawn a distinction between arms for South Africa's external defence and arms which could be used internally for enforcing apartheid. There the matter rested, almost unnoticed except by the South Africans themselves. Mr Heath and his senior colleagues were no friends of South African policy. Their handling of the Rhodesian problem while in opposition showed how anxious they were that the Conservative Party should not be identified with the white minorities in Southern Africa. Mr Heath's personal disgust at colour prejudice had emerged very clearly to those who worked with him during the argument with Mr Powell over immigration. Yet within seven months of becoming Prime Minister he found himself at the centre of a highly dangerous dispute in which Britain appeared to be joined with South Africa against the Commonwealth.

It is not for me to trace the story of this imbroglio. During the last months of 1970 I was brought into it occasionally and for only a few hours at a time. This was indeed the pattern of my work. Suddenly an issue would take the centre of the stage for a day or two. During that short time I would know where each of the characters stood. I would go to their meetings, listen to their private talk, maybe draft a speech or notes for a broadcast. A vivid snapshot of the situation would form in my mind. Then the issue would disappear from my sight as suddenly as it had come. The meetings and the talk would continue, but I would no longer be part of them. Then some weeks later through some turn of the wheel I might be involved again. The characters would be the same, but their positions altered by what had happened meanwhile, often without their realizing it. I was like a photographer who takes a still picture once during each act of a play. He is not the man to go to for a complete record of the plot, but his photographs may be of interest.

So it was with arms for South Africa. The South Africans not unnaturally moved quickly to benefit from the change of government. There was a rapid and resentful public reaction. On 21 July 1970 Sir Alec Douglas-Home made a holding statement in the House of Commons. He said that the Government intended to sell arms to South Africa for external defence of the sea-routes, but was consulting the Commonwealth before reaching a final decision. The statement did not go well. Sir Alec had the charm and authority to carry it off, but no one else could have. The thermometer of unhappiness rose steadily until it reached the fever mark. Yet it seemed impossible to treat the trouble successfully.

The difficulty was one into which most Governments fall from time to time. A relatively modest and sensible change of policy was proposed. There was nothing immoral or irrational in the proposition that Britain should sell certain arms for external defence to South Africa. We had a naval agreement with her and a strong common interest in safeguarding the Cape routes. The Labour Government had seriously considered following the same line three years earlier. In a cool calm world there was no reason why Britain should not return to a policy which she had already explained to the United Nations under the previous Conservative Government. But the world was not cool or calm, least of all about

South Africa. There was a strong protest at home among liberal-minded people, and abroad from members of the Commonwealth whose friendship was important to us. The uproar was fiercer than had been expected. The damage which British interests might suffer if we followed through the new policy began to look greater than the modest benefits from the sale of equipment. So if the question had simply been one of cool calculation, the new policy might have been abandoned a few days after its birth.

But once again the world was not cool or calm. The prestige and authority of the Government were now at stake. It is no good saying that should not be a consideration. Of course it is, and always will be in any democratic society where Governments have to explain and defend their policies in public debate almost every day of the week. It is one thing to say that politicians are too slow to admit mistakes. It is another to expect them to turn public somersaults at regular intervals. The catcalls from the audience would be too great to be endured. This was particularly true in the first months of a Conservative Government which aimed at brisk, clear decisions.

The inevitable happened. Because exaggerated language was being used against the new policy, exaggerated language was used to justify it. There was talk about firm legal obligations, about the inestimable value of the Simonstown naval agreement with South Africa, about the Soviet threat to the Indian Ocean. The dispute got out of control. It consumed a vast amount of the time and energy of Ministers which could have been better employed. It bore little relation to the central purposes of Mr Heath's Government. It stirred up emotions which were better left quiet.

Naturally enough the Foreign Office were anxious to escape from the new policy, but throughout they worked loyally to help cope with its consequences. The argument simmered on. On 15 October Mr Heath went to the Conservative Research Department for a general talk with the whole department about the Government's progress and plans. At the end of a long discussion he asked them for their views about arms for South Africa. There was a chorus of criticism of the Government's line.

The following week Mr Heath flew to New York for the General Assembly of the UN. Outside Britain the ordinary conventions about who attended what meeting disappeared. I was involved in the kind of discussions between the Prime Minister and officials which did not normally come my way. I also tackled him alone. 'Talk S. African arms to EH, who is determined to go ahead and quickly. He is probably right, tho' I still don't get the strategic argument (mine is political).' It had seemed to me since August that the Government could not pull back completely without paralysing its authority.

Whitehall was by now abuzz with various plans for calming the situation. A colleague at Number Ten and I had one variant, which involved selling some arms to South Africa but also calling an international conference to discuss how South Africa could be brought to abandon apartheid. I cannot think that it was a terribly sensible idea, but it shows how tangled we were in this particular thicket. Attention was now focused on the forthcoming Commonwealth Prime Ministers Conference in Singapore. Mr Heath called a meeting at Chequers on 1 January to prepare the line which he should take in his main speech to the Conference. There was scaffolding in the Great Hall; Mr Heath's scheme for rejuvenating and civilizing Chequers was already under way. The Foreign Office officials, exaggerating my influence, treated me rather gingerly that day as a fire eater. I was constantly being taken aside and given intellectual sedatives.

We reached Singapore on 13 January after gruelling but exciting visits to Cyprus, Pakistan, India and Malaysia. 'Fly sleepily to Singapore, Hotel Malaysia – a great bureaucratic set-up of a Conference, the reverse of what the Commonwealth should be.' We were there for nine days. As we slowly worked our way eastwards to Singapore we had come to dread the Conference. In each country we visited it was clear from the journalists whom we met that arms for South Africa was the only topic which interested them. This meant that it was the only topic of which the world would hear from Singapore. The prospect of nine days in the dock was not attractive. In fact it turned out to be rather less gruesome than we had expected.

A pattern established itself. The formal sessions of the Conference were well organized and tedious. The Prime Ministers made long set speeches which were then leaked verbatim to their papers at home. 'Just like the UN (a) too big (b) no privacy (c) too formal (d) a central bureaucracy.' There is no point in holding Commonwealth meetings at any level unless they are informal. Cheerful informality, compatible with deep divisions of opinion, is the main Anglo-Saxon contribution to the art of diplomacy. Without that quality, easier to recognize than to describe, the Commonwealth would not have come into being and will not survive. Towards the end of the Singapore Conference, the Prime Ministers rightly sent away most of their advisers and met almost alone.

There was a good deal of eating, drinking and shopping. Mr Heath gave a series of meals to his colleagues. Tension about arms for South Africa was running so high that we were never sure who would actually turn up at these meals or how those who turned up would handle themselves. There would have been headlines and applause to be gained by snubbing the British Prime Minister at his own table, but nothing of the kind occurred. Instead there was a deliberate mood of noisy good cheer.

At the week-end the Conference relaxed. For Mr Heath this meant sailing with friends. For me it meant anxious hours on the same boat keeping out of the way of the boom and the ever-active crew. 'Out to Raffles lighthouse, curry and fruit and bathe and back, scorching a bit, through the mass of tankers. Evensong at St. Andrews Cathedral, skilfully done, all white and blue Gothic and sound singing plus a long-winded Chinese bishop.'

There was a mass of work to be done in the Hotel Malaysia. Meetings with Mr Heath, Sir Alec and advisers continued far into the night after the official dinners were over. During these days I saw much of Sir Denis Greenhill and Sir Burke Trend. They were in terrific form, for they were rediscovering lost pleasures of their youth. As Permanent Under-Secretary of the Foreign Office and Secretary to the Cabinet respectively, they were normally required to advise on the broad sweep of affairs while smaller men did the detailed drafting. In Singapore they were able, late at night in their hotel rooms, to recapture the delights of composing communiqués, resolutions and terms of reference. They argued over commas, invented qualifying phrases, and worried about the balance of a sentence with the recaptured zest of a Third Secretary or an Assistant Principal.

The distinction between Ministers and officials emerged very clearly. It was for Mr Heath and Sir Alec (particularly at these meetings Sir Alec) to look ahead, weigh the risks, choose between the different complicating factors. It was for the officials to convert the result into coherent pieces of paper.

It had always been certain that the British Government would not be forced by the Commonwealth out of its right to sell arms to South Africa. It was by the time of Singapore equally certain that this right would be very sparingly used. The question was whether the Commonwealth Conference, or indeed the Commonwealth, would break into pieces on this particular rock, or whether a formula would be found. In the end the formula emerged. There was to be a study group to examine the security of trade routes in the South Atlantic and the Indian Ocean. There was to be a declaration of Commonwealth principles ruling out racial discrimination. Britain was not bound to withhold arms from South Africa while the study group was at work; nor were the African states bound to stay in the Commonwealth if such arms were supplied.

It was an untidy outcome, which in logic settled nothing, but in practice took the heat out of the situation. It was reached with great difficulty. The private talks of the Prime Ministers in the final stages were friendly and restrained, but some Prime Ministers afterwards talked flamboyantly in public. This enraged Mr Heath and affected his handling of the press. It was not for me to press a particular view on the substance of policy, but it was sometimes for me to comment on the way it was presented.

'January 21, Thursday. They spent a ragged night being abused till 4, and I doubt if there will be another Commonwealth meeting in this Parliament. EH too combative and pugnacious with press. Whole debate could re-open again on the draft Declaration. Spend middle of the day at Conference. Dinner Trend, Greenhill etc.

'January 22, Friday. March in and say firmly to EH that his press conference was too curt and that he runs the risk of throwing away effect of skilful handling earlier if he dislikes the Declaration and allows Gorton (Prime Minister of Australia) to ditch the Study Group. This is reinforced by others, and goes home. In fact the Declaration gets agreed and no one torpedoes the Study Group and he does four excellent TV interviews in the afternoon.'

Almost at once on return to Britain there was the Rolls-Royce collapse and the postmen's strike. The argument about South Africa quickly disappeared because everyone saw that it led nowhere. The Government neither renounced its policy nor sold any significant arms. The Russians did not interfere with the trade routes. During the European negotiations it was found that our Commonwealth relationships were still in good repair. The whole issue turned out an irrelevance. Like so many bitter arguments in politics, it just dissolved with the passage of time.

My most vivid memory of the Singapore Conference has nothing to do with arms for South Africa. Mr Heath gave a dinner to mark the success of Lord Carrington's negotiations for the five-power Commonwealth force to help safeguard Singapore and Malaysia. The five Prime Ministers met on HMS *Intrepid*. The ward room was crowded but the meal excellent. Particular pride was taken in the red roses on the table and the commemorative silver ashtrays. After dinner the Marines beat the retreat on deck in cloudy moonlight. The White Ensign was slowly lowered against the background of the low black hills of Johore and the grey warships anchored alongside. In theory we were celebrating the start of a new venture. In fact the evening was a calm good-humoured elegy for empire.

CHAPTER FIVE

BRITAIN FINDS A ROLE

The thread of Europe ran consistently through Mr Heath's political career. It had been the theme of his maiden speech in the House of Commons. It had been at the time of General de Gaulle's veto in 1963 the occasion of his greatest setback, and yet of his breakthrough into public notice. At the moment of his election as Leader of the Conservative Party in 1965 he was still known above all as the man who had tried to negotiate Britain's entry into the EEC. It was a theme to which he returned constantly during the years of opposition which followed. There could never have been any doubt that Mr Heath as Prime Minister would do his utmost to succeed where Mr Heath as chief negotiator had been frustrated.

During the period from 1961 to 1975 British membership of the EEC was a matter sometimes for angry debate between the political parties, and sometimes for agreement. Peace or conflict at any given moment depended mainly on the current posture of Mr Harold Wilson. Having no particular views on the subject, he treated it as a function of his relationship with his party. He was prepared to play many parts – the enthusiastic partisan of Europe, the cautious friend, the sceptic, the bitter opponent. Several of the parts were played more than once over these fourteen years as circumstances seemed to require. Yet at all times the actor was ready to explain at great length that his lines had never changed. Anyone who considers soberly the characters of General de Gaulle and Mr Wilson must marvel not that Britain entered the Community so late, but that she ever managed to enter at all.

During the spring of 1970 the political parties in Britain were outwardly almost at peace over Europe. General de Gaulle was dead. The Labour Government was again moving cautiously towards negotiations for British entry, as it had in 1967. In this they were supported by the great majority of the Conservative Party. Both party leaderships were wary of the state of public opinion at home and conscious of dissent within their own ranks.

Both therefore laid much stress on the need to negotiate a reasonable bargain. Both argued that only when the results of the negotiation were known would it be right for Britain to take a final decision.

Beneath this agreement on the surface lay an important division on tactics. The Foreign Office and Mr Heath had drawn different lessons from General de Gaulle's veto of 1963. The Foreign Office saw that France alone was the obstacle. The other five members of the Community were in varying degrees on our side. The Foreign Office therefore aimed to isolate the French further and to build up the pressure on them from inside the Community so that in the end they would be forced to let us in. These tactics appealed to the native instinct of rivalry between Britain and France which was as deep-rooted in the Foreign Office as in the Quai d'Orsay. Incidents during the late sixties such as the Soames affair, when the Foreign Office leaked to the Five an account of a private conversation between our Ambassador in Paris and President de Gaulle, only make sense if one remembers this ancient bitterness between the two great diplomatic services of Europe. Labour Ministers went along with these tactics. Mr Wilson was dismayed by the Soames affair, but he seems to have made no serious attempt to question the analysis which gave rise to it.

To Mr Heath this analysis was nonsense. He was remarkably free from bitterness against the French, who had confounded him in 1963. It would be a great mistake to suppose that he was ready to give the French whatever they wanted. On the contrary he saw them as tough negotiators with whom we would need again to bargain toughly. But he understood what the Foreign Office appeared to ignore, namely the real structure of the European Community. The French had the veto, and on the question of British entry had already used it once. There was no question of them accepting British membership just because the Five wanted us in. Only if the Five had threatened to destroy the Community might the French have wavered. There was never a real chance that this threat would be used or believed. Therefore if Britain wanted to enter it was to the French that we should pay attention. We must gain friends in France and outmanoeuvre our enemies. We must deal patiently with the French arguments, trying to meet those which had substance and to confound others which were merely propaganda. We must not try to organize the Five against France, for that was the best way to ensure that the French would again frustrate us.

This difference of approach was illustrated by several incidents between 1966 and 1970. For example there was the Congress of the European Movement organized by Mr Duncan Sandys and others in the Hague in November 1968. For me the Congress was redeemed by Mr Harold Macmillan and the marvellous flow of anecdotes to which he treated us in the lounge of the Hotel des Indes. The public proceedings were not such fun. Mr Heath made a speech in which he said there could be no Europe without France. Immediately he had sat down I was set upon by one of the Foreign Secretary's private secretaries in a towering passion. He honestly believed that we had let the side down. Peter Kirk[1] and some others of our own keenest Europeans were also dismayed, though more quietly. No one ever explained how you could realistically hope to build Europe without France. It had just become an article of faith that the French were impossible.

Mr Heath decided in the spring of 1970 that he should assess for himself in Paris and Bonn the prospects for the new negotiations for British entry, towards which the Labour Government were lumbering. So we flew to Paris on 6 May. The first engagement was lunch with the British Chamber of Commerce in the Bois de Boulogne. It was not an appetizing lunch, but ducks swam on the lake, and the chestnuts were in flower. Not all Mr Heath's speeches were good, for reasons soon to be discussed, but this one was excellent. There was no rhetoric. It was a sober and compelling statement of the reasons, still valid today, which were moving Britain towards the Community. It was also a warning of the difficult negotiations which lay ahead. Britain was asking no favours. 'We are not seeking shelter in the Community from the storms of the outside world. We have lived and thrived in that world among those storms for many centuries, and we can do so with equal success in the future.' But there was now an opportunity to break down the old barriers between European nations, and Britain and France should take that opportunity together.

On 6 May the date of the General Election was far from clear. It was two days later that Labour did unexpectedly well in the borough elections, making it almost certain that Harold Wilson would go to the country at once. In the words with which he ended his speech, Mr Heath was trying to help the future British negotiators, whatever their party.

[1] Later Sir Peter Kirk and leader of the first British MPs to serve in the European Parliament.

If it is the sober calculation of the Six that it is in their interest that Britain should join wholeheartedly in their enterprise; if they believe that with Britain they can accomplish purposes which without Britain are beyond their reach – then they must show themselves ready to allow Britain, and indeed the other candidate members, to join the Community on terms which are tolerable in the short term and clearly and visibly beneficial in the long term.

You as leading businessmen in both countries will, I know, agree that nothing could be more mistaken than to gain short-lived advantages by loading on to Britain burdens which her people will refuse to bear.

It is precisely the readiness of the Six to undertake negotiations in this spirit which is questioned by many in Britain today. So long as this readiness remains in doubt, so long will public opinion in Britain remain sour and uncertain. No one who has experience of these matters can be surprised that the prospect of yet another attempt at British entry, without any assurance of success, is regarded without enthusiasm.

For we should be clear that these are not only, or even essentially, transactions between Governments. Whatever the Government in power in Britain, I do not myself believe that Parliament will approve a settlement which in the opinion of its members is unequal and unfair. In making this judgement they will have in mind, as is natural and legitimate, primarily the effect of entry upon the standard of living of the individual citizen whom they represent. Nor would it be in the interest of the Community that its enlargement should take place except with the full-hearted consent of the Parliaments and peoples of the new member countries.

The phrase 'full-hearted consent' later fell victim to Mr Wilson's talent for distortion. It was endlessly paraded alongside the election phrase about cutting price rises 'at a stroke' as an example of Tory duplicity. Read in context, the sentence clearly implies that the decision on entry would be taken by Parliament, which would even more than usual be conscious of public opinion. There was certainly no thought in Mr Heath's mind of a referendum. What was in his mind was the evidence that British public opinion was sour towards Europe. He was warning the Six that they could not push Britain too far.

After the General Election of June 1970 negotiations got under way, prepared for the first few weeks by Anthony Barber and then conducted by Geoffrey Rippon after Barber became Chancellor of the Exchequer. Good progress was made, but it became clear that, as had always been expected, the major political decision still had to be taken in Paris. President Pompidou, the heir of de Gaulle, was in effect being asked to reverse de Gaulle's veto. There was nothing in the negotiations themselves to help him. The transitional concessions already obtained by Mr Heath in the abortive negotiations of 1962 were refined and in some cases extended by Mr Rippon. But more basic difficulties for the French remained. The British still perversely spoke the same language as the Americans, and sailed about in Polaris submarines. They were still a major industrial country which was likely to challenge the operation of the common agricultural policy. They still had strong Commonwealth connections. They still encouraged, or at least allowed, foreign countries to hold sterling balances in London. These painful attributes, which had so distressed the General in 1962/3, were still present in 1970. The political problem before President Pompidou was therefore a real one. The only way to solve it was to persuade the President that Britain was by vocation a country of Europe. Since the problem was public and political, the act of persuasion had to be public and political as well. The only person who could accomplish it was the British Prime Minister. That was the reasoning behind Mr Heath's visit to Paris in May 1971.

The negotiations had taken place against a background of doubt, even hostility, in this country. The opinion polls suggested that most people were opposed to our entry. A majority in the House of Commons would be needed for entry, and it was by no means secure. The ordinary arithmetic of the Conservative Parliamentary majority did not apply. It was my job as Political Secretary to make sure that these considerations were not lost to view in the whirl of diplomacy. I wrote a minute to the Prime Minister on 22 April, which included the following:

> An Anglo-French Summit at the end of May or early June would set the stage for what we hope would follow. I think it is true that your visit to Germany helped to lift the issue out of the bread and butter rut, and the visit to Paris would do the same.
> I think the following points would have to be made:
> a) You should not go to Paris because of some emergency in the negotiations, or because of failure to make any progress at the May meeting. You do not want to appear the *demandeur*. Indeed, reasonable progress in May might be put forward quietly as a pre-condition for a Summit.
> b) Your talk with the President should range across the world, and not be simply concerned with the negotiations.

c) Because of the high political content of the visit a great deal of attention would need to be paid to matters of form. For example, the French could be encouraged to organize special occasions and courtesies. We should aim at a result which is glittering as well as substantial.

The purpose of that visit was essentially simple, but neither Mr Heath nor President Pompidou was a simple man. Both had a love of detail and a passion for complicated information. I do not know how the preliminary briefing sessions at the Elysée were organized. At Number Ten they were held in the garden, where for hours on end the Prime Minister sat under a tree, dunking biscuits in tea. Experts were produced individually and in groups, experts on cane sugar and New Zealand butter and the sterling balances. They each had their session under the tree, while ducks from the park waddled amorously across the lawn, and over the wall on the Horse Guards workmen banged together the stands for the Queen's Birthday Parade. Ancient arguments were not entirely stilled. 'PM cross with FO for, he thinks, anti-French mutterings. This is part of the old reputation which still dogs them.'

On 14 May, after yet another briefing in the garden, a small advance party flew to Paris. It consisted of three senior officials and myself. We dined with Sir Christopher Soames at the Embassy. There was great advantage in having as Ambassador in Paris at that time a man of such political experience, with a markedly political turn of mind. Professional diplomats love the sheer range of problems in a negotiation such as this. They are always finding a fresh nuance, a further possible distinction, another hypothesis to be tested. The politician must have a rougher mind. He has to discard and simplify. He accepts that he will sometimes miss something important, that he will make judgements which he will regret. But such judgements have to be made if anything is to happen.

So Christopher Soames, a politician turned ambassador, ranged across the field of negotiations, and was sure that sterling was the main point of difficulty. It was not a new point, but it carried particular weight with the banker who was President of France. What would be the effect on the Community of admitting a new member whose economy was influenced by the fact that it still acted as banker to a large part of the outside world? Of course there was more than a touch of envy on the French side, but later events have shown that the question was reasonable. Christopher Soames said it would be our Becher's Brook.

Next day we went to the Elysée to go through the agenda with the President's team. Outside on the terrace we could see the President being interviewed by a BBC *Panorama* team, who of course had no idea that we were there. We dealt principally with Michel Jobert, later Foreign Minister, later still and more surprisingly the founder of a strongly nationalist break-away political party. Jobert was small, dark, witty, and most friendly, but he in no way prejudged the President's attitude. It was clear that all those briefing sessions had been necessary. The Prime Minister's visit would not be a formality, but a precise and detailed negotiation.

I was on the fringe of the actual visit, required to appear at meals and help with drafting, but otherwise free to gossip in ante-chambers and see old friends. The Prime Minister had a super-fluity of senior advisers. On 19 May, the first night, we dined again with Christopher Soames. 'Gold and white room, and lobster, and windows open to the lighted trees. The Knights in full cry, especially on sterling.' The next day there was a good deal of walking up and down both at the Embassy and the Elysée. I took tea at the Hotel Lotti with a senior British journalist who tried to persuade me that Harold Wilson was firmly committed to Europe and would never vote against entry. Meanwhile, the great men strolled and talked, and talked and strolled again. We, as base mechanics, wanted to know what had actually been decided. Was New Zealand butter still an issue? How far had they got on sterling? The news was scanty and slightly disturbing. 'It emerges that the great men have got through the agenda in high good humour without settling anything of importance. As C. Soames says, this won't do.' There was a magnificent dinner at the Elysée, with a mass of pink roses in the Salon des Fêtes. 'Then the Jobert group again upstairs among the tapestries, and we were dismayed to find how little had been finally decided.'

In this we were mistaken. We misunderstood the process. The French say that the absent are always wrong. In a different sense, the absent tend to believe that those present are wrong. This is particularly true of officials hanging about on the edge of a summit conference. We tended to think in terms of an orderly agenda, with items ticked off one after another. This was not what was happening. The President and the Prime Minister were immersing themselves in the problem as a whole, testing the possibilities and each other's intentions and political quality. The answer would come, not piecemeal problem by problem, but all together at the end, Yes or No. The preparatory work had been enormous, the omens were favourable, but there was still a chance of failure.

The agenda items provided the material of the discussion, but its essence was different. Mr Heath showed President Pompidou that the time had come to reverse the veto pronounced by President de Gaulle. Only Mr Heath can now say how this was done. It certainly was *not* done by giving way on every point raised from the French side or accepting every French analysis. President Pompidou was a serious man; he had to be convinced, not flattered. He had to believe that Britain was coming into Europe not out of despair, not to make trouble, but as a determined and capable partner.

The winning round of President Pompidou was probably the greatest single feat of Mr Heath's premiership. In these talks he repaired the errors of twenty years of faulty French and British policy. A few years more and the errors might have been irreparable.

The next day, 21 May, was grey and wet. The pieces fell into the right pattern. By the late afternoon the Prime Minister and President made their joint declaration of agreement on British membership in the Salon des Fêtes. President Pompidou had bravely chosen for this demonstration the room in which his predecessor had pronounced the veto.

The success seemed complete and was, indeed, a triumph of diplomacy. But it was becoming clear that there was another battlefield waiting at home.

It is worth recalling the background. There was no question in 1971 of a British referendum on Europe such as was held four years later. Both Mr Wilson and Mr Heath had specifically ruled out a referendum during the 1970 election campaign. There was no doubt in anyone's mind that the decisive votes would be taken in the House of Commons. There would be a major debate on the principle of entry on the terms achieved, followed by a vote. Assuming that entry was approved in principle, after an interval there would be a Bill making the necessary changes in our own law.

The Whips and the soothsayers were therefore busy counting votes in the House of Commons. Their task was not easy. The Labour Party leadership moved smartly to oppose entry on the terms negotiated by Mr Rippon and Mr Heath. There was no reason whatever to suppose that they would have gained better terms had they remained in charge of the negotiations, a point made embarrassingly clear by two of their previous negotiators, Mr George Brown and Mr George Thomson. This did not prevent the Labour leaders from denouncing the terms as intolerable.

In the long run the attitude of the Labour leadership was vitally important, but in the short run it was clear that the Whips of both parties were in difficulty. This was an issue so important that when the time came the requests of the Whips would be shouted into the wind. Those who wanted to hear would do so; others would abide by their own convictions. There was a sizeable band of Conservatives who had opposed British entry honourably and consistently. There was also a band of Labour MPs who for many years had distinguished themselves in the European cause. Neither Mr Heath nor Mr Wilson nor their Chief Whips could hope to influence the core of these two groups of rebels.

There were however a number of Members not wholly committed to either side of the argument. Most of these would probably follow the lead of their Party, Conservatives for and Labour against. But there were plenty of whom this was uncertain. No one knew what they would do. Informed people guessed very differently. Bill Galloway of the US Embassy, who knew a great deal about British politics, told me on 15 June that he thought the majority for entry would be 25. On the same day Robert Rhodes-James's guess was 5 or 10. There was certainly no comfortable margin. The vote was in the balance.

It would depend to a large extent on how MPs gauged public opinion. The polls suggested fairly consistently that public opinion was hostile or apathetic, though the figures were rather more favourable to membership in 1971 than in 1970. The Government itself had already fallen into a pit of unpopularity. On 28 May it lost the Bromsgrove by-election to Labour. The experience of the Macclesfield by-election the same summer showed that some Conservative Associations thought for a few months that they could best weather the storm by choosing an anti-Market candidate. Against this background the faint-hearted would not lack arguments.

In the early summer Ministers discussed timing. If the negotiations ended in agreement during June, when should the result be put to the House of Commons for a vote? There were a few hotheads, such as myself, who wanted to push ahead as fast as possible. I wrote a minute to the Prime Minister on 7 June.

As you know, the Chief Whip's present inclination is that there should not be a vote in principle before the summer recess. This is because he rates so highly the danger of appearing to rush Members of Parliament before they have had time to listen to their constituents. My own view is that the dangers of allowing Members to go away for the recess without taking a vote in principle are probably the greater, and that it would be worth sitting well into August for this purpose.

My worry was not that Members would turn against Europe as they bustled among their constituents during the months of August and September. It was that the Party Conferences, Labour and Conservative, might turn sour if they considered the question before Parliament had given a lead. However, as usual the Chief Whip, Francis Pym was right, and Ministers decided on a short postponement. The House of Commons was not being asked to pronounce on the terms until October. Meanwhile Ministers were to make a powerful effort to take public opinion by storm.

The public debate on Europe in the summer and autumn of 1971 was a dress rehearsal for the referendum campaign four years later. Then, as later, there were contacts across party frontiers between the pros and the antis. Then, as later, a mass of arguments, sound and unsound, were tossed into the balance on both sides. Then, as later, public opinion rallied in support of entry.

The difference lay in the attitude of the Government. In 1975 the Prime Minister Mr Wilson, with his Foreign Secretary and his Chancellor of the Exchequer, stayed out of the campaign as far as they decently could. Towards the end they took a hand and gave the 'Yes' case a mild blessing, but they were anxious throughout to minimize the divisions in their own Party. In 1971 by contrast the Prime Minister Mr Heath and his colleagues were in the forefront. They recognized that it was an uphill task. An elaborate and far-reaching campaign was planned, of the kind which Conservative Central Office prefers and at which it sometimes excels. I spent most of the morning of 6 July there:

This is eve of European battle. It has a satisfactory feel, as of an army well prepared with its charge and cannonades, now impatient for action against odds – whereas the General Election was a defensive battle, won but fought defensively in fog at a time and place of the enemy's choosing.

The Prime Minister launched the Government's effort in the House of Commons with a statement on 7 July. The next day he

made a Ministerial broadcast. On 12 July he held a press conference at Lancaster House. On the whole the campaign was going
well. On 26 July I wrote, 'The European offensive has captured
more positions than we thought possible at this stage, and there is
a danger of slip from now on.'

In August Ministers disperse, and things tend to go wrong.
There are two views about the politics of August. In Opposition
before 1970, and again after 1974, we were convinced that August
was a good month for governments. Parliament was up, there
were no awkward debates or questions for Ministers, it was a
difficult month to hold public meetings. Ministers could go on
making announcements and gaining headlines, but an Opposition
had few chances. In government, however, we held the opposite
view with equal firmness. August, we concluded, was a treacherous
month for government. Senior Ministers, even senior officials,
snatched a few days' holiday, and at once disaster struck. Because
the Whitehall machine was not in gear, it took weeks instead of
days to grip a new situation. In 1971 this certainly happened with
Upper Clyde Shipbuilders. The miserable question whether and
then how this firm should be helped or reorganized dragged
through the late summer, embarrassing and weakening the
Government. There was also much Irish business. On 6 September
'EH with Lynch at Chequers – unresponsive to other matters and
still wholly unprepared to bother with trivia like speeches,
broadcasts etc'.

During this summer recess of 1971, as Members of Parliament
sought the views of their constituents on Europe, another question
began to emerge. As early as 7 July, the officers of the Young
Conservatives on one of their visits to Number Ten had pressed
the Prime Minister to allow Conservative Members a free vote on
entry into Europe. During the next three months this possibility
was much discussed. There were good arguments on both sides.
As a former Chief Whip Mr Heath believed in party discipline. In
this instinct he was supported by another former Chief Whip, Mr
Whitelaw. As Prime Minister, Mr Heath believed that the Government should use every means in its power to honour the agreement
which it had reached with the EEC. He was supported in this by
the Foreign Secretary, Sir Alec Douglas-Home. These views, so
powerfully backed, were not easy to overcome. Nevertheless, they
were overcome, and a free vote for backbenchers conceded. This
was a turning point in the whole process of securing British entry.

The current Chief Whip, Mr Francis Pym, had no love of

anarchy and no desire at all to endanger our agreement with the EEC. It was precisely because his convictions were so solid that his argument for a free vote carried weight. It was based on arithmetic. By the second week of October the Whips had reported on the mood of the Parliamentary Party. There were, as everyone knew, a sizeable number of antis. The conclusion drawn was that, so far as the Conservatives were concerned, the whipping would make little difference. From the other side of the hill, the information was less full. There was a considerable mass of Labour MPs whose position was unclear. Many disliked the line being taken by Mr Wilson and Mr Callaghan that the terms of entry were unacceptable. But these were not on the whole natural rebels. The chances of their following their own judgement might substantially increase if there was a free vote on the Conservative side. This would be true even if Mr Wilson attempted to whip them against entry.

This was the argument carried unresolved to the Conservative Party Conference at Brighton on 12 October. I always enjoyed Party Conferences, but they are the worst possible occasions for obtaining decisions from great men. There are far too many distractions. There are speeches to be made and listened to, delegates to be entertained, journalists to be argued with into the small hours. The great scurry happily from hotel to hotel, suite to suite, restaurant to restaurant. Orderly habits of work are suspended. The volume of chatter drowns thought, and reasonable men become hopelessly disorganized. A noisy, amiable chaos reigns.

It was therefore perhaps naïve to suppose that the Prime Minister and his colleagues would decide on a free vote in time for the Prime Minister to announce it in his big speech to the Conference on the Saturday morning. The Europe debate at the Conference on 13 October, itself went very well, and there was an overwhelming vote in favour of the terms. The Prime Minister had a long and most enjoyable dinner with a group of journalists. It was impossible to turn his mind either to his main Party Conference speech or to the free vote question. Behind the scenes advisers argued about it incessantly, but that was not much use. On Friday he at last began to think about his speech, but 'the great men let the free vote founder late last night, indecisively and in weariness. This is a shame, and at the very centre there is a mounting worry about the 28th, caused by the hard and sizeable core of our antis – say 33.' 28 October was the date set for the vital vote in the House of Commons on the principle of entry into the EEC.

As so often happens, the passing of a few days changed the atmosphere. There was a week-end of reflection. Away from Brighton, people could think more rationally. Nothing substantial occurred between Thursday 14 October and Monday 18 October, but on the second date Ministers took the decision at which on the first they had jibbed. They were all conscious of a risk, but now believed it was worthwhile. The reaction on the Labour side proved them right. The leadership did not relax its opposition, but the pro-Marketeers found their courage. On 28 October the vote was taken after five days of debate.

> One only gets into Europe once in a lifetime, and this today is done in style. EH v. relaxed all day, asking for this and that. In the debate from 8 on. Enoch forceful in a set-piece way, Callaghan very adequate, Wilson in the early afternoon soporific as to two thirds, then rallying, but still well below the level of events. EH v.g., though runs a bit dry. An overcrowded House, great tension and an overwhelming majority of 112, the Labour pros having held very firm, and the free vote having paid off.

The majority of 112 was far higher than I had heard predicted by anyone. This was the crucial vote. Of course there was much weariness and uncertainty to come. The slow progress of the domestic legislation, with majorities often in single figures, the failure of the EEC to cope with the oil crisis, the renegotiation under Mr Wilson, the referendum campaign of 1975 – all these had their moments of great tension, and no doubt there are more to come. But the vote of 28 October 1971 was crucial because it cut across party lines. There had been a great danger that under opportunist leadership the Labour Party would drift into opposition to British membership as a matter of principle. That danger still existed for years to come but the vote of 28 October neutralized it for the time being. British membership can only be a success, like all major policies, if it is supported by both the main parties in the House of Commons. That support was not yet fully assured, and this for a long time weakened Britain's hand inside the Community. But the decisive vote of 28 October 1971 gave us the strength to make a start.

CHAPTER SIX

SPEECHES AND SILENCES

'Either be silent, or speak things better than silence.' Communication has always been one of the arts of government. In Britain it has never been more important than today. On the one hand, the nation has been educated in disillusion. Its underlying sense of unity, to which a Prime Minister and a Government have the right to appeal, is partly lost in the clamour of interest groups, each identifying their own cause with the public good. Politicians by their own partisan behaviour have often thrown away the right to call to the nation as a whole.

But a Government now, more than in the past, needs the support, or, at least, the acquiescence of the electorate day by day in what it is trying to do. Ministers do not communicate simply to win for themselves approval today and votes tomorrow, though that is one purpose. They need to communicate because they know that the people are not just the source of authority but a necessary ally in using authority to good effect. This is true however narrowly you draw the boundaries of state action.

Ministers often forget this need, or give it too low a priority. Others believe that they have done all that is necessary if they have had a word with a man from *The Times*. There is a rule now that any paper coming to Cabinet (and indeed any Bill coming to Parliament) should include an explanation of the cost to the Exchequer of the proposal which it contains. Donald Maitland, Mr Heath's Chief Press Officer, once suggested while we were at Number Ten that each paper should also include a paragraph setting out how the policy was to be explained to the British public. It is not a bad idea. Of course one can carry the argument too far. Communication should be the servant of policy, not the master. In the end it is not sensible to do things solely in order to be able to say that you have done them. It is even less sensible to say that you are about to do something which is never on the cards at all. But more often the error is the other way. The red boxes, the continuous meetings, the company of experts, the self-importance of office can all tempt a Minister to forget an essential question: how would I explain this if I were sitting in the living-room of one of my constituents?

It *ought* to be done through Parliament. Parliament was once, and should be again, the open forum where Ministers explain what they are about, and the elected representatives pass judgement on it and on them. Parliament *should* be the place to which people look for information and debate on public matters. It should be the focus of their attention. In its Victorian heyday, and for some time after, this was so. Moreover the prestige of Parliament gave to the individual Member of Parliament an opportunity to communicate with his own constituents in his constituency if he wanted it. A glance at the old files of a local newspaper will show what I mean. Every word which an MP uttered at a public meeting would be reported, complete with the applause and the hecklers.

Almost all that has gone. Parliament is now only one, and not the most important, means by which public affairs are brought before the public. This has happened partly for secondary reasons. Parliament was absurdly slow in allowing its proceedings to be directly broadcast. Of the limited space which it allows to Parliament, the national press makes over a large part to writers who prefer to review our proceedings from the gallery as theatrical drama or farce.

But the main fault lies not with the media but with the present temper of Parliament, which is both violent and feeble. We operate a system of partisan politics which the electorate once relished as a sport, but which is now out of favour with all except a minority of political enthusiasts. We persist in discussing complicated policies as if there were only two possible judgements, that of our own party being wholly right, the other wholly wrong. So long as Parliament behaves in this out-of-date way it will fail in its main task of controlling and influencing the executive. It will also be forced aside from its rightful place as the centre of political debate. People simply do not take seriously the toy drums and tin whistles of ordinary party politics as practised on the floor of the House. Governments will never be able safely to neglect Parliament because Parliament has kept the power to make the lives of Ministers intolerable. But until Parliament reforms itself as ruthlessly as it has reformed other institutions, Ministers will not treat Parliament as their main means of communicating with the nation.

When he became Prime Minister in June 1970 Mr Heath

needed no persuading that communication was important. He had built up in Opposition a small team of advisers in this field whom he trusted and who had served him well. There was Michael Wolff, a close personal friend who, as already mentioned, was content to be called a speechwriter but whose particular gift of weary wisdom had earned him a position of great trust and strength. There was Geoffrey Tucker, the Director of Publicity at Central Office. From outside the political world there were James Garrett, Barry Day and Ronald Millar, each bringing a special talent. There was nothing formal about this team. Different individuals were called in for different purposes. There was much painful wrestling with particular speeches or broadcasts; a good deal of wining and dining. The world was taken apart and put back together in many restaurants. All in all, it was a successful effort which proved itself in the election campaign of 1970.

It was a private effort, and those who took part sought no headlines or advancement for themselves. What they did expect was the confidence of the man whom they were trying to help. They knew that they would not get this by flattery. On the contrary Mr Heath expected, indeed insisted on harsh criticism of his own public performances from those whom he trusted. He might then turn fiercely on his critics, and there would be a shindy; but next time round they would find that the criticism had been accepted. This method of proceeding caused anguish from time to time but I think that we would all, looking back, say that it was fun.

This team were not out to create something called the new Heath, smooth, homogenized and empty. What they were trying to do was to help Mr Heath build on the strengths of communication which he naturally possessed. These were considerable. Find a group of forty or fifty serious people, perhaps student leaders or trade unionists or American journalists or Bexley constituents, and put Mr Heath among them with no microphone in sight and plenty of time ahead of him, and you might well listen to a striking feat of communication. Few political leaders can have such a range of detailed knowledge. This knowledge was combined with the belief that evidence rather than prejudice ought to be the foundation of political decisions, and that discussion among serious people was the best way of getting that evidence. The tragedy was that gatherings of this kind, which were the best political meetings I have known, could only be occasional and limited in the numbers of people they reached.

For introduce a rostrum, a microphone, an interviewer or a

few thousand people and the result could be disastrously different. The voice might change its quality. The vocabulary might become stilted, the tone defensive. The thread of the argument might be lost in a mass of detail. Instead of speaking to people, Mr Heath would too often speak at them.

In trying to cure these habits Mr Heath was not trying to create an artificial self. He was finding a way of transferring more surely into public life the natural gift of private communication which his friends knew well.

At the outset of government Mr Heath took two sensible decisions. The first was not fully maintained. He decided to keep together the small group already mentioned which had helped him in opposition. They were invited to steak and claret on his first Sunday evening at Chequers. We sat late with the Prime Minister discussing the ways in which during the next five years he should try to keep in touch with the nation. I cannot remember what was decided. I do remember accepting a lift back to London in Geoffrey Tucker's Giulia Sprint. We got lost in the first two minutes and ended up in a haystack on the Chequers estate. It was an omen. For however good his first resolutions a Prime Minister is almost bound to neglect them. Under the cares and pressures of office Mr Heath began to put aside what he had learned about communication in the painful years of opposition. He was probably better at it in the General Election of 1970 and in the European Referendum Campaign of 1975 than at any time when he was Prime Minister.

The second good decision was to call Donald Maitland back from the Embassy in Tripoli to become Chief Press Secretary. Mr Heath had thought hard about this appointment before the election. He felt that Mr Harold Wilson had made a great mistake in turning the Press Office into a political fief. A Prime Minister needs to be sure that his Chief Press Officer is loyally expounding his views, but the press also needs to feel that it is getting a fair statement of the Government's problems and intentions. It is very difficult to reconcile these two requirements. I doubt if it can be done by a political partisan. But there is a strong case for appointing someone from outside the narrow caste of Government information officers. For the Chief Press Officer at Number Ten is not only concerned with the Prime Minister. He is expected to speak for the Government as a whole, and this means co-ordinating the information output of every department.

The Foreign Office does not have a separate information service.

It staffs its News Department from the ranks of the Service as a whole, which means bringing in people who in earlier jobs have actually helped to form and carry out policy, as opposed to people who have done nothing for years except explain the policies of others. This Foreign Office practice, from which Donald Maitland had gained his experience, gives a wider outlook and enables the spokesman to speak with greater authority. Because of this background and his natural gifts Donald Maitland served admirably. It is an exposed position, and there will always be grumbles. But he came as near as anyone could to reconciling the different demands of an almost impossible job.

A Prime Minister has three main means of communication – the House of Commons, speeches outside, and broadcasts. Of these the House of Commons was for Mr Heath the least difficult. He was not an exceptional orator in the House, but he had a personal authority which when added to the authority of Prime Minister made him formidable. When tired or short of time he sometimes made the mistake of trying to plough through pages of written text. It is amazing how often through caution Ministers fall into this error. A Minister making an important speech in the House needs to give himself the greatest possible freedom. He needs to be able to give way courteously and willingly to friends and opponents who want to make a point in the middle of his speech. He may need to shorten or add to his speech as he goes along to suit the mood of the House and the advance of the clock. He should aim to slip in spontaneous asides which occur to him on his way. A Minister with a written text finds it difficult to do any of these things. He is wooden and remote, and the House will react accordingly. It is the hardest thing in the world to depart from a written text and then come back to it successfully.

Every Minister who wishes to survive works out his own technique to cope with this problem. Mr Heath usually did as he had done in opposition. The morning before a speech in the House he spent a long time alone covering small sheets of paper with copious notes in his own writing. If Government Departments had supplied a text for certain passages, that text would be boiled down into notes. The sheaf of notes on the dispatch box provided a fortified position from which he could sally, and to which he could retreat. Because he had mastered the material when transcribing it, he could abandon two or three pages if necessary without losing his way.

On the whole, though I listened to a few bad ones, Mr Heath's speeches in the Commons went well. He was not particularly nimble, but that is anyway a talent of opposition. He was at his best in presenting with clarity and force the facts and figures which pour on to the desk of a Prime Minister. Even in difficult times he was rarely worsted in debate or at question time. There was often noise on the other side and occasionally doubt on his own. The waves would sometimes close over the Prime Minister's rock-like figure, but when they subsided he would still be there at the dispatch box, not noticeably shaken or eroded.

A Prime Minister's year seen from his Private Office is a steeple-chase of speeches outside Parliament. Sometimes the high fences come dangerously close together. In mid-May for example a Conservative Prime Minister normally speaks within a few days to the Scottish Party Conference, the annual dinner of the Confederation of British Industry, and the Conservative Women's Conference. All three are major occasions.

In November the Lord Mayor's dinner at the Mansion House may come close to the debate in the House of Commons on the Queen's Speech. September is the best month for long tours and many speeches outside London, because most people are back from their holidays but Parliament is not sitting. No Prime Minister can complete this annual round of speeches without help. No Prime Minister will want to rely on just one source of help. But he quickly finds that his main difficulty is making coherent sense of the help at his command.

Suppose, for example, that the Prime Minister decides a week before a speech that it should deal with the latest set of trade figures, which are mildly encouraging. The civil service will advise against this, because it is dangerous to generalize from one month's figures. The Prime Minister overrules them. There is good news and he wants to give it. Then the Department produces a draft full of percentages and qualifications. Every sentence is so hedged with intricate dependent clauses that no mortal could get his tongue round it. The Prime Minister, having three days in hand, says 'Try the Conservative Research Department'. They produce a fiery piece, again full of percentages; the good news in the figures is a triumph for Conservative policy, the less favourable ingredients are the result of the Government's lamentable inheritance from his predecessor. The Prime Minister says 'check those figures'. The Department, its nose out of joint, produces a different set of figures, with an annex of incomprehensible explanation. The Prime Minister says 'Try X', who is outside Government, and has seen no figures at all. With twenty-four hours to go, X produces a draft beginning: 'Britain is astir again. You can feel the sap rising. Not before time. And not without cause . . .', and so blithely into a mass of monosyllables and a minimum of verbs. All these drafts are carefully docketed and flagged by a Private Secretary and put before the Prime Minister the night before the speech, with a polite minute saying that the Press Secretary needs the approved hand-out by noon next day.

This is a caricature, but only just. The preparation of speeches can get out of hand unless the Prime Minister takes a grip at each stage. I understand that Mr Wilson used to do this. The chief complaint against Mr Heath's methods of work was that often he did not. I seem to have spent all my working life drafting speeches for other people, and I hate it. It becomes almost intolerable when one has no clear guidance on what is needed. Over and over again we would start a day or a journey with a major speech looming at the end of it for which we were not ready. On 20 November 1970 the destination was Torquay. 'Lunch, and he sleeps and reads yachting papers, and only in Somerset does he for the first time read the draft. Speech is OK just, without much of him in it, and he is tired.' On 9 March 1971 it was the North East. 'Dictate a bad speech for Newcastle. It is really impossible to do these things without an inkling of what he wants to say.' The same theme recurs month by month. Nor was I the only or chief sufferer.

We often puzzled over this. It was not that Mr Heath failed to understand the importance of speeches. He knew the magic of words, and often talked about it. In fact I believe this was the trouble. He was a perfectionist. We served up adequate drafts, which he saw were only adequate. It would take him hours to transform them – but the necessary hours were never there. They were swamped by meetings, and yet more meetings. So at the last minute the adequate draft was looked at, reluctantly approved, and unenthusiastically delivered. Next time of course would be different; but next time turned out much the same. It was a mystery and a tragedy that a man who possessed such a talent of exposition could not find a working method which turned it to good effect.

The most important speech in the year of the Leader of the Conservative Party is made at the end of the Party Conference in October. This had always been a nightmare, not for Mr Heath, but for those who tried to help him. In the old days the Leader of the Party had descended on the chosen watering place in a first class carriage a few hours in advance, delivered his speech, acknowledged tumultuous applause, and been whisked again into heaven. Mr Heath, by contrast, stayed at the Party Conference from beginning to end. The Metropole Hotel at Brighton and the Imperial Hotel at Blackpool will always have a peculiar hold on our memories, if not our affections. Mr Heath went occasionally to the conference hall itself and sat on the platform during important debates. Most of the time he spent in his hotel suite. 'Working on his speech, I suppose?' people would say. 'Yes, indeed,' we would reply. We wished it was true, but feared it was not. Certainly there was a great deal of activity, for whether on sea or land, at work or theoretically on holiday, Mr Heath never actually rested for a moment. At Blackpool and Brighton there were colleagues to be seen, there were constituents and journalists to be entertained in restaurants, there were menus and guest lists to be studied. There were foreign visitors to be received, the Conservative leaders of great city councils to be asked for advice, headwaiters to be given autographs, and each evening a string of receptions to be attended. But there was no speech. There was always about to be work on the speech, intense inspired work which would make it the best speech ever. But Wednesday drifted into Thursday into Friday, and still there was no speech. There was just a steadily accumulating pile of suggested passages from various well-wishers – the Research Department, outside help, Michael Wolff and dozens of others.

Then on Friday night, when a long dinner was finally over, work would begin. Mr Heath would sit at his desk and compose his speech. He would accept some of the suggestions piled before him and discard others. He would demand new facts, figures, quotations. He would write long passages in his own hand on small sheets of notepaper. The confusion of accumulated paper would some time around midnight threaten the whole enterprise. But at his elbow like an accusing angel stood Michael Wolff. It became a tradition that Michael should undertake this task. Patiently he guided, suggested, criticized into the small hours. Then Mr Heath would go to bed saying, 'I shall be up early to finish the speech.' But Michael Wolff would be up a great deal earlier. By now, three hours before Mr Heath was due to mount the rostrum, perhaps two-thirds of the speech would be approved. Secretaries with long experience and strong nerves would be hammering it out in final form. In the morning, as each page was cleared, we snatched it and sprinted down the hotel corridor to the typing room. Finally Michael Wolff emerged with the last page saying, '*Habemus papam*, we have a speech.' While Mr Heath dressed, the secretaries worked desperately against the clock. With the minimum of noise they numbered or renumbered the pages, tagged them together, slammed down telephone receivers, filled wastepaper baskets (there were never enough) with discarded matter. Finally, a few minutes before the car took Mr Heath to the conference hall the speech was ready. No copy for the press or colleagues, no time for briefing; but the Leader had a speech. He himself remained calm throughout. Immediately after the speech there was always a private party for those who had helped. Never was champagne more strenuously earned.

What ended as a ritual had begun as a nightmare. Mr Heath's Party Conference speeches in Opposition before 1970 were treated by the press as tests of a shaky leadership. He appeared to be on trial before one of the most difficult audiences a man can have, the troops whom he commands. This was particularly true in 1968 and 1969 after the breach with Mr Powell. There were vociferous critics, it is strange to recall, who believed that Mr Heath lacked determination and character. Gradually by his tireless visits up and down the country Mr Heath strengthened his hold on the loyalty of active Conservatives outside Parliament. Their miraculous success together in 1970 sealed this pact of loyalty, which then survived with remarkably little damage until Conservative Members of Parliament chose a new leader in 1975.

After 1970 the Conference speech, though still important, was no longer crucial. The ritual however survived. The 1970 Conference was at Blackpool. On Tuesday 6 October: 'Imperial Hotel, shoddier than I remember, thronged with friendly faces. We are as usual nowhere with the speech.' Wednesday 7 October: 'We make no real progress with the speech, and this bothers me.' Friday 9 October: 'It looks as if we may have exorcized the demon of the conference speech' but still 'no text at all'. Saturday 10 October: 'EH's quiet revolution speech – not brilliant, but revealing as more his own than most, and the emotional context is terrific.'

That of course was the point. Conference speeches do not always read well, but they are not meant to be read. For once the audience was more important than the report afterwards. I used to dislike listening to these speeches because I felt so involved in them. I could not bear to sit down, but used to move uneasily from one position to another at the back of the hall, testing the applause and the look on people's faces.

In the end each Conference speech succeeded. They did not change the course of history. But they assured the audience of the courage and sincerity of their Leader, and they gave the Leader another year during which he could as necessary ask hard things of his Party.

Speeches in and out of Parliament will always be important, but they are not now as important as broadcasts direct by radio or by television. Here the first and crucial decision for a Prime Minister on each important occasion is whether to broadcast at all. My diary is full of small wrangles on this question. When anything went wrong, or indeed right, the instinct of the Party was usually that the Prime Minister should broadcast. We would then analyse the advantages and drawbacks of the different forms. He could do a Ministerial broadcast as Prime Minister – but then under the rules the Leader of the Opposition would have the right of reply the following night. Or he could make a party political broadcast in a slot already reserved for the Conservatives – but that would make it a Party not a national message. Or he could accept one of the pending invitations to take part in a current affairs programme – but much would depend on the competence or prejudice of the interviewer. While we argued over these pros and cons, the Prime Minister and his official advisers would stay cautious and uncommitted. Often the broadcast would be delayed or not take place at all. Often we on the Party side would become extremely cross. Once I wrote: 'There are always excellent reasons for missing boats, and we are getting good at it.' Looking back I think that I was frequently wrong in this recurring argument. Prime Ministers should not broadcast too often. Each such broadcast should be an event. They should not, on the other hand, leave too long a gap between broadcasts, because broadcasting like cricket or tennis needs constant practice. They should broadcast when they have something positive and important to say, not whenever there is some sudden crisis which puts the Government on the defensive.

Different arguments apply to other Ministers and to the Party as a whole. At a moment of real difficulty Ministers are busy. The situation may be changing daily, and it will always be safer to stay silent than to broadcast and say the wrong thing. Junior Ministers, who could be invaluable at such moments, are usually told to keep quiet, in pursuit of the silly but traditional policy of burying in the ground such political talents as they possess. Backbench Members of Parliament cannot easily get the necessary briefing. So a Government can drift dangerously until its output is less in quantity and quality at a critical moment than the output of its opponents. This is a particular danger for a Conservative Government. Trade union leaders are usually ready to broadcast. At the national level they are well-briefed and articulate. The same cannot always be said of employers either in the public or private sector. Too often, poor innocents, they believe that silence is golden. Having kept silence for a few days they realize too late that they have been forced into a corner by public opinion based on the output of their adversaries. On industrial and economic matters the caution of Ministers and the silence of employers were often during 1970–4 no match for the concerted effort of the Labour Opposition and the trade union movement.

This was a recurring theme of my own notes to the Prime Minister. Here is a typical example from the spring of 1973.

> PM
> You may like to glance through this monitoring report of the week-end's radio and TV, with the immense coverage of the industrial and political situation.
> I think the position is:
> a) Ministers are broadcasting more often and better than before.
> b) Some of our backbenchers are good, others damaging: on average a good deal worse than Labour MPs.
> c) The TUs are *much* better than they used to be, as the monitor reports on Page 3.
> d) The nominal employers hardly ever appear and are bad when they do. This means that in the present situation we tend to be outnumbered; the need for continued exertion by Ministers is correspondingly great.

As the situation in 1973 became more desperate this weakness persisted. Under the heading 'Miners – publicity' I wrote to the Prime Minister on 12 November. 'The Party are still deeply worried about this. The press is good. But on radio/TV the National Union of Mineworkers have it mostly their own way. On Thursday Gormley appeared ten times, and was only matched once. Despite assurances the National Coal Board are almost silent. Ministerial appearances have been fitful – and not good.' I then went into the case of a Minister whom 'the Party thinks has an instinct for avoiding danger. Could you please have a personal word with him? A

Minister ought to appear each day on one aspect or another if we are not to lose ground.'

It was easy to understand why deeply tired and anxious men should not want to broadcast. To broadcast successfully is almost as difficult for a Minister as to speak in a foreign language. Some have the knack, others learn painfully or not at all. Indeed a different language *is* what is required. A Minister reads paper after paper on his subject, bustles from meeting to meeting. He learns the jargon, the statistics are banged into his brain. He expresses himself in the language of that subject – and each subject quickly breeds its own language. After a particular meeting, say with the trade unions, he agrees to broadcast. He has an hour or two, perhaps only a few minutes, to think about the broadcast. He has to forget his detailed knowledge, forget the statistics, obliterate the jargon – and turn his thoughts and policies into the language of the living-room and the saloon bar. No doubt during those precious minutes of preparation some well-meaning lunatic of an adviser will peer round the door with a brief containing a fresh batch of statistics or a new refinement of jargon.

We tried to brief Mr Heath in the opposite direction, towards simplicity. On one occasion: 'words to avoid, because meaningless to the majority of audience: regressive, relativities, anomalies, unified tax system, productivity, threshold agreements, deflation, realignment.' These were of course all current jargon which we knew would trip all too easily off any Minister's tongue once he was deep into argument with the interviewer. 'Also avoid percentages where possible . . . people do not understand references to Stage 1, 2, 3, unless explained.' And so on. I cannot pretend that we were brilliantly successful with this advice. We would have fared better with a man who had more time to think his way back into everyday language. In this respect we would have fared better with a superficial man who cared only for the politics of an argument and not for the facts and figures. Mr Heath believed that people deserved the evidence, and, by God, they were going to get it. It sometimes made for hard pounding. Most broadcasts on politics now take the form of an interview rather than a statement straight to camera or microphone. This has been one of the main shifts in methods of communication during recent years. The reason is fairly obvious. People are not used to hearing speeches in their living-room. The same voice talking continuously for more than a minute or two creates a strain. They are however used to conversation. They find it easier to absorb in-

formation and argument if it comes to them in the form of dia-
logue. They dislike violent disagreement because that too is
unnatural in most living-rooms. The interviewer who picks a row
with a politician, or a politician who picks a row on television
with another politician, will soon find from his postbag that
he has made a mistake.

The commonest criticism of political interviews is that the
politician does not answer the question. Sometimes this is fair –
though politicians probably give as straight an answer to an
awkward question as, say, a professional footballer or club
manager. But there is a previous point: what right has the interviewer to insist on his particular set of questions? On what principle have these questions been asked and others not asked?
Anyone can find out the qualifications and the prejudices of a
particular politician. What are the qualifications and prejudices
of a particular interviewer? They are not so easily discovered. A
politician can justly, it seems to me, use an interview to put
across the arguments which he thinks are important on the subject
being discussed. If he is skilful he can bring these in as part of
an answer to a question which is put. But in any case he has the
right when he leaves the studio to feel that he has said what he
wanted to say, so that people can judge. The divine right of
interviewers to govern a discussion is not absolute.

Of course there are occasions when a straight broadcast is best.
At a moment of major crisis there is a general instinct that the
Prime Minister should speak direct to the nation. A Prime
Minister must first speak direct to Parliament, for that is a necessary convention of the constitution. Now that Parliament has
finally allowed itself to be broadcast, a statement to Parliament is
also a statement to the nation, and Parliament will be the main
beneficiary. But in 1970–4 Parliament was still in purdah. A
new device was needed if the Prime Minister was to dispense with
interviewers and journalists and speak simultaneously through
the media to the people.

That was the justification for Mr Heath's exceptional press
conferences at Lancaster House. There was one already mentioned
on Europe and another on the second stage of the incomes policy.
17 January 1973 – 'Quite a day. Briefing 10.30. Robert and William
Armstrong and a mass of detail on the Stage 2 White Paper,
coffee and biscuits. I try to guide it on to crude politics, and am
rebuked. Redraft opening statement . . . To Lancaster House
where in splendid white and gold room before a throng from

around the world, EH performs admirably for an hour. Opening statement over-long, but the whole tone firm and calm.'

But whatever the techniques he uses, a Prime Minister will not communicate well unless he has a reasonable relationship with the communicators. There seems to be a regular cycle in the life of most politicians. The aspiring politician loves to communicate, and he likes journalists and broadcasters. At the next stage the politician still enjoys communicating, but he is enraged because what he says is not used and what he does not say gets banner headlines. He abuses editors to their face or rings up proprietors behind their back. He is above all anxious to put the record straight. Many politicians do not progress beyond this second stage. The third stage is weary disillusionment. Since the newspapers always get it wrong, since journalists and interviewers are mere butterflies of the moment, trivial or malevolent beyond cure, it is not really worth bothering a great deal about them. Only history will put the record straight. Mr Heath was not quite in this third stage, but sometimes not far off. He was rarely angry with the media, certainly much less so than some advisers, but he rarely warmed towards them. There were individuals of course whom he trusted and whose company he relished. There were occasions when he unexpectedly shone. The BBC knew a thing or two when they staged a *Panorama* programme with him on Europe in the Metropole Hotel at Brussels. It was perhaps the best broadcast he did as Prime Minister. He was often at his best with European or American journalists, for he carried no scars from them, and they came from outside the intimate world of British newsgathering.

Somehow it should be possible to get these relationships right, or, if not right, better. The component parts are really not too bad. We have a set of journalists and broadcasters who, though often sensitive about any criticism of themselves, are on the whole talented and honourable. We have a set of politicians of whom exactly the same can be said. We have a general public which is better equipped to digest information than ever before. Yet politicians and communicators scratch and scrawl unnecessarily against each other's profession. They neglect the obvious fact that each profession is necessary to the other. When that relationship improves the public will be better served.

CHAPTER SEVEN

GROWING PAINS

Mr Heath and his colleagues brought Britain into Europe. Everyone who worked closely with him before 1970 knew that was the first, though not necessarily the more important of the two aims which he had set for his premiership. The other was even more ambitious. It was to free Britain from the constraints which had held back her economy since the war, so that she could achieve those levels of stable growth which were already becoming normal in Germany and France. In this he and his colleagues for the time being failed. It is with this effort and failure that the rest of the present book is concerned.

It is not for me to write the history of this struggle, for the reason, which seems adequate, that I do not know the full story myself. There is much that is still dark about economic policy in 1970–4, including some matters which become more obscure as controversy tries to illuminate them. The senior Ministers concerned, in particular Mr Heath and Lord Barber, have remained silent except on some points of detail. In this they are probably wise – not because they have nothing to say, but because the last four years would have been the worst time to say it.

History is a good judge, but she needs time to collect her thoughts. The early evidence placed before her rarely turns out to be the best. At that stage partisans are still using the immediate past to make points about the present. The first proper history of the period 1970–4 is probably still five or ten years off.

The aim of what follows must be limited. I took part throughout in one aspect of the struggle, namely wage disputes in the public sector. I was involved in the final drama of the second miners' strike, and in the decision to hold an election in February 1974. It seems best to concentrate on describing how these events felt at the time. It will be for others to assess the importance of these footnotes to the main story.

But first there is something to add about the declared aim of Government, namely steady economic growth at a higher rate than had hitherto been achieved in Britain. For it is now widely held that economic growth is *not* the right central aim for Government. In the first place we can now see that some resources necessary to growth are finite. Unless for example we can switch to non-fossil sources of energy more quickly than seems likely, the industrialized world may run short of energy in a generation.

Secondly, inflation has become the most feared enemy. For a few months in 1974-5 we in Britain suffered inflation at 25-30%. Even now, we can see how inflation at less than half that figure undermines our society. If inflation continues even at this reduced rate (still far more than that of more successful countries) many of our free institutions and voluntary activities will in a few years stand diseased like elms in a hedgerow, reminding us for a few years more of a better past, until they are finally toppled. If economic growth is bought through high inflation, then the price is too steep.

There has also developed a moral argument against economic growth. We are told that in the industrialized West we already have enough. The present Bishop of Winchester, for example, argues cogently in his book *Enough is Enough* that we are seduced by commercial advertising into wanting the dishwasher, the second car, and the foreign holiday. This piling up of possessions and material satisfactions impoverishes our real life. We should resist the temptations and accept a stationary standard of living which would give us a more rational happiness, and leave more of the world's resources for those who do not yet have enough.

This last line of argument runs directly counter to what I guess to have been Mr Heath's personal driving force through his political career. One of my first expeditions with him was to Aviemore in Perthshire. There was a Party meeting of some kind, and Sir William McEwan Younger, later Chairman of the Conservative Party in Scotland, wanted to show him the hotel and sporting complex which his company had helped to build there. But the most vivid impression which Mr Heath carried from Aviemore came from the skiers to whom he spoke on the slopes. They had come in Minis from Tyneside and Clydeside and the Lothians for the week-end, hiring their skis and boots, the sons and daughters of parents who would have no more dreamt of a ski-ing holiday than of owning a yacht. And that of course was the next example, vivid before Mr Heath's eyes every time he took his boat *Morning Cloud* from her moorings. Anyone who doubts the results of economic growth in a free society should visit Chichester Harbour or should stand on the bank of the Hamble on a Sunday evening in the summer to watch the line of small boats returning up the river. This is not the accumulation of useless possessions, or the heaping up of privileges for the few. It is an extension to the many of a recreation, a stretching of the mind and body, which was previously limited to a tiny group of the rich.

Then there is the clinching example. Anyone who wants to understand Mr Heath's economic policy might well read his book on music. The son of a small builder, born in 1916 many miles from London, found by hard work a way into the world of music. The opportunities were limited, and many must have flagged where he persisted. Now that way is easy for all. Not because the music or the musicians themselves are better, but because a combination of new technology and economic growth has brought to almost everyone who wants them radio, television, long playing records and cassettes. Here again, even the most egalitarian bishop must surely recognize not a deadening but a quickening of the human spirit.

The most telling arguments which Mr Heath could use in favour of his growth policy came from his own background. He hardly ever used them. He disliked bringing his private activities into public debate because he felt that to personalize the argument was to cheapen it. It was an attitude which did him credit, and cost him dear. If he could occasionally have thrown his whole self as we knew it, the private *and* the public man, into a particular argument at its crisis the result would have been formidable.

Economic growth in Mr Heath's mind was not just a question of enriching the ability of the individual to find and use his own talents. The social services were hungry giants which gobbled resources which could only come from growth. If there was no growth, education, the National Health Service and the other services would begin to wither. That argument like many others, was just an argument in 1970–4; now it is a reality. We have grand new hospitals which we cannot afford to open because the running costs are too high. We have education skimped and many social services cut. This is not because the taxpayer has been spared. On the contrary he has been loaded with new burdens which are unprecedented and intolerable. It is because we have run out of economic growth. Are we more contented, more virtuous as a result? We ought to be, according to those who argued earlier that we had enough growth already for our spiritual good. But of course we are not. Because there has been no economic growth we are *less* generous towards our own poor (including our immigrants), *less* able and willing to buy goods from the poor in the rest of the world, and a *less* useful member of the international community.

In Mr Heath's belief the instrument for achieving economic growth was the private enterprise system. He was as emphatic in this belief as Mrs Thatcher after him. Though different in style his speeches and hers do not on this point differ in content. It is not through state organization and direction but through the play of individual skills and the taking of individual risks that real prosperity is created. There can be no argument on this between members of the Conservative Party. But this does not mean that Conservatives need to approve everything that the private enterprise system throws up. Because we believe in freedom we do not have to applaud every choice which free men and women make. The political difficulty about freedom is that it gives disagreeable people the chance to flaunt their habits in a way which is offensive to their fellow citizens. This fact is the *raison d'être* for many socialists; but it cannot be helped. Mr Heath, though not a puritan in his personal tastes, had a puritanical approach to work and to idleness. Baldwin said that one of the least enjoyable duties of a Conservative leader was to listen to lectures on the laziness of the working class from men whose idea of a hard day's work was to spend an hour blowing greenfly off their roses with the smoke of a cigar. Mr Heath would have agreed.

The Lonhro affair in 1973 gave rise to Mr Heath's famous phrase about the unacceptable face of capitalism. The first explosion on that occasion was subterranean. It occurred during his speech at the annual dinner given privately each year during the Scottish Party Conference at Perth by the President of the Scottish Conservatives. As already noted, Scottish Party Conferences have a special flavour. It is partly conveyed in my diary for 11 May.

Early to Turnhouse. With EH to the Kincardine Police College. This is well organized and interesting among cedars. Classes and lunch and he plants a sequoia, and off on the familiar road to Perth. The ritual of many years unfolds. Listen to an abysmal economic debate, wound up well by P. Walker. Work on chunks of speech. Dinner, 6 elaborate courses . . . EH explodes. The ugly face of capitalism, class distinctions, the essential responsibility of management. Not very well composed, but passionate – and they don't understand a word. An office bearer gets up and talks about the sole and the sweet, and tickets for the Agents' dance at £2. The Lord Provost contributes 50 pence, and rejoins the Party in emotional terms. EH presented with a bottle of North Sea Oil. It is all an Evelyn Waugh occasion.

It is a shame that Evelyn Waugh never wrote a real political novel. He could certainly have done justice to the ease with which an audience hears what it expects rather than what is said. I am sure that many of Mr Heath's audience went home that night from the Station Hotel at Perth with a comfortable glow, warmed by the passion with which, so they supposed, the Prime Minister had defended free enterprise. Next day he repeated his criticism in more measured terms in his public speech at the end of the Conference. Muddleheaded people began to say that a Conservative Prime Minister should not criticize capitalism. It is precisely because the Conservative Party accepts the merits of capitalism that it is qualified to criticize its workings. For the same reason it should listen with particular care to what businessmen say about its own policies and performance.

What businessmen had been saying in the years before 1970 had been clear enough. They blamed the policies of stop-go for the failure of the private enterprise system to deliver prosperity in Britain on the same scale as elsewhere. No sooner was there a prospect of expansion, no sooner did the home market look favourable, no sooner were boardrooms beginning to contemplate higher investment, than the Government would announce that there was a balance of payments problem which could only be solved by squeezing the home market. The car industry in particular had stressed that exporting was not fun if the home market was periodically restricted by government action. Businessmen argued that politicians must break out of this cycle. Only when business could see a high and steady level of demand at home as well as abroad would they set about re-equipping their factories and modernizing their methods with confidence. Only in these conditions could they bring down their unit costs, and so provide the country with a firm foundation for yet more growth.

It was accepted that there were dangers at the beginning of this road. At the outset, before the new capacity was installed and unit costs reduced, a policy of expansion would mean a sharp rise in imports. Politicians should not lose courage at this point, for it was a barrier which had to be pierced. It was argued that this might have happened in 1964–5 if the General Election of 1964 had not occurred at the wrong moment. The Labour Government had taken office just at the time when the Chancellor of the Exchequer's, Mr Maudling's, policy of expansion was at its moment of greatest danger. Misinterpreting the situation, they declared there was a crisis and so produced one. If instead of jamming on the brakes they had kept their nerve the balance of payments would anyway have righted itself in 1965, the investment would have come through, and we would have continued at a higher level of prosperity. So according to many businessmen, the lesson of the sixties was that politicians must keep their nerve and sustain through a period of danger a long-term policy of expansion.

In his pamphlet *The Growth Merchants*, Mr R. Pringle has analysed in much greater detail the pressure for a growth policy from the opinion-formers. He writes in a polemical 'I told you so' tone which has some justification, but I think he underrates the importance of the advice given by businessmen themselves.

In its earlier versions this doctrine was familiar to Mr Heath from his time as President of the Board of Trade in 1963–4. Later it was dinned into his ears as Leader of the Opposition from 1966–70. It appealed to his underlying belief in courage and a readiness to take the long view as the prime qualities of politics. Nothing in his own life had come to him the easy way. The same had been true for Britain, and would be again. There were risks in a policy of sustained growth, but it was the only policy which had a hope of long-term success.

This point is crucial to any understanding of the events of 1971–2. It is nowadays a commonplace that Mr Heath and his colleagues lost their nerve at that time because they were frightened of the political consequences of unemployment. I cannot write of arguments used at Ministerial meetings which I did not attend. Nevertheless I believe that the common explanation is exaggerated. It is true that Mr Heath felt strongly that the modern Conservative Party had to shake off the spectres of the past, of which mass unemployment was the most formidable. No one of Mr Heath's background and generation could easily dismiss rising unemployment as a statistical fiction or as unimportant. Despite this, the political advisers of the Government were at all times more concerned about inflation than about unemployment. We knew how the 1970 election had been won – we knew how the next election could be lost. At meeting after meeting we concentrated on the course of prices. No other consideration had in our minds anything like the same political importance.

The fundamental reason for the policy of expansion begun at that time was not fear of unemployment but determination to achieve growth. The Government believed that although the free enterprise system must be the chosen instrument for achieving prosperity, governments could and should help. Their action could not be confined to holding the ring. There would from time to time be occasions when Government should actively move in to remove an obstacle or unravel a tangle. Their aim in such positive intervention was not to take freedom away from the private firm or the individual citizen, but to make it possible for them to exercise their talents to better effect.

This of course leads to the heart of the debate inside the Conservative Party during recent years. The debate will ebb and flow. In different forms it will probably go on for ever. We have seen a revival of the view that all such intervention by Government is mistaken and unconservative. This criticism of the approach taken by Mr Heath and his colleagues in 1970-4 goes well beyond the statement, now generally accepted, that a Government cannot check inflation while letting the money supply expand unchecked. It extends to a proclamation that at all times in all matters, apart from defence and foreign policy, the free market is a better guide to human happiness than the action of Government. There is of course nothing new about this doctrine. It was commonplace in the two middle quarters of the last century, though then identified with the Liberal rather than the Conservative Party. It underlay Cobden's hostility when Lord Shaftesbury tried to help children working in factories. We can read it vividly expounded in Miss Woodham-Smith's book on the great Irish famine. It was clear to the genuinely humane officials of the 1840s that it would be cruel and wrong to interfere in any decisive way with the operation of the free market which dictated that thousands of Irish should starve. We can read it in Mrs Gaskell's *North and South*, or in Dickens's *Hard Times*, where the phrases of Mr Gradgrind and Mr Bounderby only slightly caricature a good deal of what we read today about the absolute virtues of the market. It was dislike of this philosophy, by then become stale and uninspired, which drove the young Harold Macmillan and many others into revolt against the Conservative Party between the wars, and which led in the view of many to the terrible defeat of that party in 1945. Since then the intellectual pendulum has swung, and much the same doctrine reappears, freshly presented and in many respects appealing. I can quite understand how to a Conservative student of today the era of Macmillan and Heath may seem as half-hearted and compromising as the era of Bonar Law and Baldwin seemed to Macmillan and Heath when they were young.

But fashion is dangerous. There is another strand of thought about the role of the state which has a rather stronger claim to be called conservative. It has been spelt out many times, but in recent years not perhaps better than by Mr T. E. Utley in an article reviewing a book by Professor Hayek which appeared in the *Daily Telegraph* on 10 January 1977. Mr Utley was and is a trenchant critic of Mr Heath's Government. He believes that much of what they did was wrong-headed and damaging. He praises Professor Hayek warmly for his rejection of most recent legislation. But he goes on to reject an absolute approach.

Why then do the ancestral voices of Toryism persistently warn me against Dr Hayek? In a nutshell, because his rigid ideology, which rests firmly on the view that the free market is a panacea for nearly all politically curable ills, exaggerates one of the great truths about politics at the cost of neglecting the other. In its concern for liberty, it disparages the importance of social cohesion.

I simply do not believe that if society decides that some evil produced by the spontaneous forces of competition (e.g. mass unemployment in an area like Ulster, afflicted by civil disturbance, or the destruction of the farming industry) calls stridently for governmental action to temper it, that action is bound to prove disastrous, however prudently and deliberately it is conceived and carried out.

Like other ideologues, Dr Hayek lets the baby out with the bathwater. Though he is the most effective critic of the collectivist nightmare into which we have been plunged by politicians who believe in administration rather than politics, it is not to him that a renascent Tory Party must look for its philosophy.

With Burke I recall that there are very few things about politics which can be rationally affirmed to be universally true; and with Disraeli I prefer 'the liberties we enjoy' (or, to be precise, those we used to enjoy) to the 'Liberalism' which Dr Hayek professes.

It is a fair comment on Mr Heath and his colleagues that they did not spend much time justifying their actions in terms of ideas. There was a great deal of policy, but after 1970 not much philosophy. But had they wished to do so they would have spoken in words not unlike Mr Utley's. It is possible to criticize the abolition of resale price maintenance, which was Mr Heath's main legislative feat before 1970; or the industrial policy which led, through the nationalization of Rolls-Royce and the drama of Upper Clyde Shipbuilders, to the Industry Act 1972; or the final and most reluctant resort to a statutory incomes policy in 1972 and 1973. These were all major interventions by a Conservative Government in the working of the economy. Several arguments can be brought against each of them, but not, I believe, that they were in principle unconservative. A Conservative Government will in practice always hold itself ready to act in the national interest when things go badly wrong with the economy. It is most unlikely at the moment of crisis to use the argument that it can do nothing because its ideology says that nothing can be done.

But in politics personalities and personal predilections matter as much as ideas. In his book, *The Politics of Power*, Mr Joe Haines criticizes Mr Heath as a civil servant's Prime Minister. This is untrue if it means that civil servants shaped his ideas. The civil servants who worked most closely with him would, I think, laugh ruefully at such a notion. But it is true in the sense that Mr Heath had a high regard for the civil service. I sometimes wondered if this regard would have been so great if he had served longer as a backbench MP, or if he had not spent so much of his Ministerial apprenticeship in the Foreign Office. To some extent all senior Ministers are vulnerable in this way. The Private Secretaries in their own office and the very senior officials whom they themselves see day by day are usually people of high calibre. They talk well, listen attentively, know the world, and express themselves quickly and fluently on paper. This is particularly true of the Foreign Office. It is rather too easy to suppose that the whole public service is peopled with such agreeable paragons. In fact it is not. The traditional vices of bureaucracy are delay, excessive devotion to detail and a rigidity of thought which is reflected in authoritarian attitudes towards the citizen. These vices exist – usually at the lower level where policies are executed. The citizen is in touch with these levels, so is the conscientious backbench Member of Parliament, but the Minister is not. At the top of the civil service there is order, reason and reassurance – until the roof caves in.

Because of his justified respect for his senior advisers Mr Heath tended to exaggerate what could be achieved by new official machinery. If he had been somewhat more sceptical he would, for example, have been less ready to believe that the Department of Trade and Industry was competent, even with the outside advice provided, to use the sweeping new powers to spend money selectively which were given them in the Industry Act 1972. More important, he would a year later have pinned less faith on the Relativities Board, which was expected to sort out, in the light of common sense and natural justice, the endless anomalies and unfairnesses which exist between the pay of different groups in a fast-changing free society, and which are inevitably increased by the early, more rigid stages of a statutory incomes policy. This is not an argument against the principle of either the industrial policy or the incomes policy. Personally I believe that both were at the time inevitable. But a little more scepticism about machinery would have been wise.

Rising prices were the main preoccupation of Conservative Central Office during the period 1970–4. Sir Michael Fraser, the wise and philosophical Deputy Chairman of the Party, together with the Directors of Organization, Publicity and the Research Department, used every opportunity open to them to keep inflation at the top of Ministers' minds.

It is worth describing what these opportunities were. At the end of Mr Macmillan's Government in 1963 there had been a general feeling in the Conservative Party that Ministers had drifted out of touch with their own supporters in the country, partly because there was not enough regular contact between Ministers and Central Office. I do not know how far this was true, though there must always be a temptation for Ministers after years in office to become too Ministerial for their own good. Certainly there was a determination in 1970 that this should not happen again.

Machinery abounded. Indeed its whirring sometimes made it difficult to think. As Political Secretary at Number Ten there were several meetings each week which I was expected to attend. On Monday there was the Liaison Committee, which met in the splendid office of the Lord President of the Council in the old Treasury building. On Tuesday there was Sir Michael Fraser's Tactical Committee at Central Office. Early on Wednesday there was the Chairman of the Party's large weekly meeting, at which almost every senior dignitary of the Party had a seat if he was willing to get up early enough. Thursday and Friday were blessed in having no regular meetings.

Of these bodies the most important was the Liaison Committee. The Lord President of the Council (first Mr Whitelaw, then Mr

Prior) held a key position in Government. Having no department
of his own he was asked to take the chair of important inter-
departmental committees. As the Leader of the House of Commons
he knew the Government's plans, and had a shrewd idea of the
time-bombs which at any given moment are ticking in the major
departments of Whitehall. Both Mr Whitelaw and Mr Prior were
well known and well liked in the Party. They were thus the right
people to preside over the Liaison Committee. Its membership
shifted from time to time, but in principle this was a meeting at
which the Lord President explained to senior officials of the
Party the Government's view of the current scene. In return the
Party officials had a unique opportunity to question and grumble.

But machinery is not enough. The Prime Minister and his
colleagues were usually patient and courteous in listening to
advice from the Party, but those who gave the advice began to feel
that it carried less weight. This always happens. In opposition
senior Party officials are often the chief advisers of the Party's
leaders, on policy as well as presentation. The Party wins an
election and the leaders move into Whitehall. They are still the
old friendly faces, sensible and easy to reach. Everyone is exhorted
to keep in touch with everyone else. At first all seems fine. Then
the Party becomes aware of other voices speaking to the Minister,
other influences at work. The curtain twitches, there is someone
concealed behind the arras. Facts become difficult to get, promised
papers do not arrive, Ministers though still friendly are evasive.
The Official Secrets Act and (far more important) the entrenched
habits of Whitehall turn the familiar friend into an occasional
acquaintance. Until of course a general election is called – then it
is the civil servants who retire, and for a glorious week or two it
is to the Party veterans that Ministers turn for news and advice.

I recorded some of this more prosaically in one paragraph of a
paper sent to the Prime Minister in August 1971 under the title
'The Party as auxiliary to Government':

> This machinery is, I understand, better thought out than anything
> which existed under the last Conservative Government, except
> perhaps in its final year. Nevertheless, there is a general impression at
> all levels within the Party that this administration is in fact less
> politically conscious than its Conservative predecessor. I suspect that
> the Lord President would agree with this. There seems to be greater
> difficulty in getting Ministers to think politically about their daily
> problems. As a result there is a tendency in the Party to criticize the
> Private Offices and Press Departments of Ministers who sometimes

appear to keep them in a sort of cocoon, over-protected from the outside world. There is something in this criticism as applied to Junior Ministers. This is bound to be a continuing struggle in which the more lively elements in the Party have a definite and important role to play as goads and stimulators.

Looking back over these innumerable meetings, looking back indeed over the whole of my time at Number Ten, there is no doubt which subject swallowed up most of my working time. The Government's handling of public sector disputes was the dominant theme. Of course there were many months on end without such a dispute, when we worried about other things. There is a law which provides that subjects suitable for worry expand to fit exactly the time set aside for that purpose. We were paid to worry, and there were many hours set aside each week for this activity. But there occurred through these years a series of major disputes, and when they occurred it seemed clear to us that they were more important for the future of the Government than anything else that was going on.

Nor did this concern depend on whether there was or was not a statutory incomes policy in force at the time. It amazes me that people still occasionally argue about whether or not the Government should have an incomes policy, without realizing that the answer must be yes so long as a large part of the nation's work force is in the public sector. Where the Government is the ultimate employer it must have a policy for deciding the salaries and wages of the employee. One can argue what that policy should be. One can argue whether or not that policy will or should affect the private sector. But any Government has to decide how it proposes to handle wage and salary claims in the public sector.

The difficulties which the Government found in this task between 1970 and 1974 were immense. The Labour Government tranquillized this area in 1974 by giving everyone too much money regardless of the consequences, and thereafter by a skilful exercise in persuasion. But the underlying problem which Mr Heath's Government found has certainly not gone away.

In the nationalized industries the Government is the ultimate employer. It provides the finance, and in the public eye is responsible for the policy. Indeed the plain man asks what on earth is the point of nationalization unless the Government can be held to account for what is done. A Government is usually trying to restrain excessive pay settlements in the public sector. It does not matter particularly whether it claims to be doing this in order to keep down public spending, or to prevent price rises, or to respect a general incomes policy which it is laying down for the nation as a whole. The justifications of the need for restraint will vary from time to time, but the need remains. This is a strong argument, among others, for reducing the scope of the public sector, but no one supposes that this can be quickly done.

So the difficulties have to be faced. For although the Government is the ultimate employer it is not the negotiator. It is not the Government which sits across the negotiating table with the miners or the railwaymen; it is the National Coal Board and British Rail. The Government can in most cases (though not in the important case of local government employees) intervene with a formal directive. It can also, to some extent, influence matters behind the scenes. But in practice neither of these is a very useful weapon.

In our experience the negotiating habits of the different nationalized industries were much the same. They worked out roughly how much they could offer their employees within the Government's current pay policy. They then offered this amount at one go to the union. If enquiries were made at this early stage by Ministers, they would explain that this was a subtle tactic. They were dazzling the union with their generosity, they were making an offer which could not be refused. The offer was of course promptly refused. Accustomed to negotiation, the union denounced the first offer as an insult, and began to talk of industrial action. At this stage Ministers would be alerted. But already they were faced with the choice between a poor settlement and a terrible one. Increasingly, but too late, they were drawn into playing the hand, a job for which they had few qualifications.

It sometimes happens in politics that a simple fact escapes busy Ministers. It seemed to me that this was so during several of these public sector disputes. The fact was that the men concerned usually had no incentive to settle. It was rare for them to suffer much financial loss through the industrial action which they were taking. Strike pay or tax rebates or supplementary benefit for their families took the edge off real hardship. There was an offer on the table. It was never withdrawn; it could only be improved. Statements about the long-term damage to their industry cut little ice. Once industrial action had started, the odds were usually that it would continue for some time, and that the outcome would be expensive.

Public opinion, so people said, was the joker in the pack. In a public sector dispute both sides played for it. If the Government found public opinion hostile, then it was unlikely to persevere for very long in opposing a claim. If a union found public opinion hostile, this might or might not affect its stand, depending on the actual power of that union to disrupt the economy. So the metaphor of the joker in the pack is inexact. The Government *had* to have public opinion on its side if it was to hold on. Some unions could manage without. The postmen were affected by public opinion, the miners were not.

Public opinion usually went through a cycle. It began each time by supporting the Government's general efforts to check inflation. People understood the connection between, for example, the wages paid to electricity workers and the price of electricity. At the first touch of industrial action there was often a polarizing of public attitudes. A deluge of telegrams, letters and telephone messages would now cross my desk. They came to me because they were mainly from active Conservatives, but at this stage they were probably fairly representative. 'Stand firm: we're behind you.' 'Not a penny more.' 'No surrender.' People like to see an issue suddenly simplify. After weeks of complicated negotiations and arguments, there are suddenly two sides, each arrayed under its standard. No more committees, no more blurred edges, but a trumpet call and a trial of strength. It is all very lamentable of course; but it is also quite exciting. I expect that is how Cavaliers and Roundheads felt when, after the weariness of the Long Parliament, they found themselves at Edgehill. But of course industrial relations are not exactly like that. Military metaphors are dangerous, because military battles usually end in defeat or victory, whereas industrial 'battles' usually end in compromise. People who have thought in terms of defeat or victory feel betrayed, and that is always a dangerous emotion.

The trade union leaders were usually effective in public argument during a dispute. They were well briefed and they knew which arguments to use. It is always possible in any industry, however highly paid, to find hard-luck cases. For some reason or another there will always be someone somewhere in that union whose take-home pay is miserable, whose wife hardly knows where to turn, whose children will have no Christmas stocking. If such there be, the union will find him, so will the *Daily Mirror*, so will the television. Then the camera switches to a plump-looking person from the employer's side with an unsympathetic voice who conducts the argument in terms of abstract percentages. Or, even worse, does not switch at all. One of our main difficulties was to get the Government's case put. The employer in the nationalized industry was almost always reluctant to say anything. He did not want to sour the atmosphere or prejudice the outcome. These considerations never seemed to occur to the trade union on the other side of the table. But in any case the head of the nationalized industry was not the right person to do the job. For the Government's case always went wider than the particular industry in dispute. It was the case for the taxpayer and the consumer, the case against inflation which had to be put. Only Ministers could do this. But Ministers were not the principals in the dispute. It was not to them that the radio and television producers went for an interview. They were not handling the negotiation or familiar with all its details. They too were reluctant to go over the parapet. So we used as already noted to agonize over monitoring reports which showed a striking preponderance of broadcasts by the trade union side to the dispute.

Then public opinion might well begin to shift. There was inconvenience or worse. There were no trains or no electricity. There seemed no end to the struggle. The sense of drama quickly disappeared. For a day or two it is quite fun to light candles or walk to work; not for very long.

People who had urged the Government to stand firm would now criticize it for being obstinate. The press, responding quickly to the change of mood, would pick on any suggestion of compromise. Mr Whitelaw used to watch out for the first use in the press on each occasion of the phrase 'light at the end of the tunnel'. When he spotted it he would groan loudly. From then on the Government would be under pressure to sacrifice its policy to the need of the moment.

During the final dispute with the miners I received a call asking me to go and see a prominent industrialist. He had an urgent message for the Prime Minister about the strike. I took a taxi down to his office in the City. This was the head of a big company, renowned for the robustness of his right-wing views. He was, as he often observed, a down-to-earth practical person. He put to me his own plan for settling the dispute. It showed that he had no inkling of what the dispute was about. His plan involved giving the miners very large sums indeed under a flimsy disguise. I was a message boy. It was not for me to remark that if the

Government had accepted his plan, it would have been the signal for a wage explosion – such as occurred a few months later. I muttered some words of caution and went my way. For that man, running a business which was suffering from power cuts, the short-term need to settle had become paramount. Eventually his advice was more or less taken by the incoming Labour Government – and industrial production three and a half years later was still below what his company and the others were achieving during the power cuts and the three day week. Perhaps there is something to be said for down-to-earth practical people occasionally considering the long term.

Eventually in any dispute the time would come to compromise. After all that had been done and said in public, this was extra-ordinarily difficult. The compromise was like a pot into which would be thrown the original claim, the financial state of the industry, the Government's counter-inflation policy, the damage being done by the dispute, and the state of public opinion. These were the ingredients; it remained to find a cook. A court of enquiry, a parcel of wise men, a law lord – they took their turn at the task. The Government was by then almost powerless, yet in the eyes of the public it would be responsible for the dish which emerged. It would certainly have to digest the consequences. But it was virtually impossible to reject the dish once the prestigious cook had been employed. The Government was, in practice, at the mercy of those who had been summoned to prepare the compromise. Sometimes the result was from the Government's point of view tolerable; more often it was tolerated only because it had to be. It is impossible to understand the handling of the final dispute with the miners without grasping what the Government had previously had to endure at the hands of outside arbitrators.

It would be tedious to describe each of the disputes in turn. Obviously each had its own characteristics. One of the first, with the electricity workers in December 1970, was typical enough. By 7 December I was writing 'Cold, and the electricity go-slow hits harder and quicker than expected'. The next day 'A bad day. It is clear that all the weeks of planning in the civil service have totally failed to cope with what is happening in the electricity dispute; and all the pressures are to surrender.' That night I dictated a short minute for the Prime Minister's black box:

ELECTRICITY DISPUTE

From the political point of view the bare bones of the situation seem as follows:

1 A settlement of the dispute at over 12% would be a defeat for the Government's policy against inflation so severe as to be decisive. A new policy would have to be devised fairly quickly with all the attendant disadvantages.

2 There is at present no effective incentive to the workers to return to normal working. Neither the loss of overtime nor the vague pressure of public opinion is likely to be effective.

3 The inconvenience being suffered by industry and the public is above the level which they will find tolerable over an extended period, unless the Government are seen to take action.

4 If the Government take no action and simply go on saying that they will not connive at an inflationary wage settlement the mounting inconvenience will probably lead to very strong pressures for surrender.

If the above points are correct the Government needs to find quickly, i.e. this week, a means of action which will (i) appear decisive to the public and (ii) at the same time provide some inducement to the workers to resume normal working. The situation is sufficiently serious to warrant overriding the inhibitions which traditionally govern the handling of these matters.

One possibility would be for the Government to instruct the Electricity Council to withdraw the existing offer of 10% by, say, 14th December. This would satisfy the requirements for Government action set out above.

Already most of the elements are there. Early next morning, Tim Kitson, Donald Maitland and I called on Mr Heath upstairs in the flat while he was still in his dressing-gown. We said that if the Government treated the electricity dispute as a crisis it had the chance of a victory, not otherwise. The Prime Minister involved himself much more closely, and the situation changed. By the week-end Mr Robert Carr as Secretary of State for Employment was in the thick of negotiations for a court of enquiry. On 14 December the unions agreed to accept a court of enquiry and end their industrial action. It was treated as a success for the Government. But there were lessons to be learned, which became painfully familiar over the next three years.

PRIME MINISTER

December 14, 1970

Wage Claims

There is a chance that the Government's success in handling the electricity dispute can be used to transform the general situation. For the first time public opinion has clearly and unmistakably made the connection between a particular wage dispute and the general struggle against inflation.

A great prize awaits the Government if it can turn this dramatic happening to long-term account.

This will not happen automatically. It will surely depend on

a) a successful outcome to the court of enquiry. Paradoxically the Government's very success so far has made a 12 per cent settlement look decidedly unattractive. But this point needs no labouring.

b) a fresh look at plans for future public sector disputes, designed where possible

i) to bring the negotiating body concerned to offer a good deal less at the outset than has hitherto seemed practicable.

ii) to ensure that in future effective and practical pressure can be exerted against industrial action before it begins, e.g. by making offers conditional on there being no such action. This is entirely rational, since industrial action obviously limits the ability of an industry to pay.

iii) to examine again the practical side of contingency planning for mitigating the effects of any future disputes. This did not look impressive this time, and some things which were said at the outset to be impossible (e.g. warning of cuts) are now being done. (Surely the Official Committee is too large, and you need a small group of officials under an energetic Minister, not holding too many meetings.)

c) to look again at private sector claims. For example the clothing and footwear wages council, where, if I understand right, there may be a case for a government directive to head off a big award.

It would be a great pity if the impetus of these last days were lost and all these matters lapsed back into routine and orthodox consideration. The Government need not worry so much about being seen to take a hand. A good deal may now be possible which was ruled out before. But this, I fear, will only happen if there is continuous stimulation from the top.

But of course much depended on what the court of enquiry actually recommended. In February 1971 it came up with a complicated award considerably higher than the Government had hoped.

If the result of that electricity dispute was ambiguous, there was no doubt in anyone's mind about the result of the miners' strike in February 1972. It was disastrous. The Government attempted a stand, the life of the country was severely upset by power cuts, the work of compromise was entrusted to a distinguished judge, Lord Wilberforce, and his award was far too high for the national interest. This award caused an upward pressure on wages which after many efforts in other directions could only be checked by the statutory incomes policy introduced nine months later. Even more important, this setback, which the Prime Minister and his colleagues made no attempt to disguise, made it impossible for them to accept a similar outcome of the next dispute with the miners in 1973/4.

It would be wearisome, and very depressing, to go through the course of the dispute of 1972 in detail. The elements were by that time familiar. It occurred at a moment when Ministers had a great deal else on their minds. On 30 January thirteen people were killed in the 'Bloody Sunday' riot in Londonderry. For the next two months, until the declaration of direct rule on 30 March, Irish affairs were in the melting pot. Ministers went back to first principles on Ireland. A completely new policy had to be devised, and new people found to run it. I do not know enough of this effort to write about it, but watched from the sidelines it was one of the most impressive things which the Government did. Inevitably it swallowed up many days in the diary of senior Ministers. More than that, the subject had a very high emotional content. To those who dealt with it, including the Prime Minister, it was clearly the most important matter of the moment.

There was also anxiety about Europe. No one could be sure whether the European Communities Bill (the legislation taking us into the EEC) would pass. The Labour pro-Europeans, who had performed so gallantly in the vote on the principle of entry four months earlier, were a doubtful quantity when it came to the Bill itself. The second reading debate was held on 17 February, at the crucial stage of the miners' strike, and of course the Prime Minister had to speak. He was tired, but his speech was adequate, and there was a majority of eight in favour of the Bill.

So as usual everything was happening at once. These weeks of the 1972 miners' dispute were the worst of all. There seemed no way through. On 11 February: 'The Government now wandering vainly over battlefield looking for someone to surrender to – and being massacred all the time.' That evening I went to Witney for my adoption meeting as prospective candidate for the new Mid-Oxfordshire constituency. Power cuts had begun in earnest. There were 250 people, all enthusiastic. They did not yet realize that the Government had no cards left. On 18 February: 'From frying pan to fire. Wilberforce gives an immense amount to miners, which they show signs of rejecting.'

At the final meeting that evening at Number Ten Mr Heath persuaded the miners that they had won enough. Throughout he had been remarkably calm and self-possessed. The facts of power in Britain were against the Government. They were also against any realistic economic policy. There was at that stage no statutory incomes policy. Somehow, as he said in his broadcast ten days later, we had to find a better way.

During the next few months much thought went into this. Ministers were anxious on practical and political grounds to avoid a statutory incomes policy. They had no illusions about the difficulties which a statutory policy would involve. The next dispute was on the railways. In June 1972, I wrote another note to the Prime Minister:

At the last strategy meeting at Chequers there was general consent for the view . . . that so long as inflationary pressures are serious, the Government must retain the right to intervene in public sector pay negotiations . . . The trouble is that this right is at present exercised under conventions which can make it ineffective. The Government's views are transmitted to the employers, but the latter retain a tactical independence which can frustrate the Government's intentions. For example, we are faced in the rail dispute with the difference between an excessive settlement, if all goes well, and a very excessive settlement, if all goes badly. This, as I understand it, came about because the Board went to the limit of their mandate *without* achieving a settlement.

Might it not be possible for the Government to *call in* negotiations when necessary and handle them themselves? This would only occur in major disputes where a major national interest was at stake. It would have the consequence that existing offers by the employers would be withdrawn, and negotiations would start again from scratch. From the presentational point of view the situation would be clear-cut and would be a powerful incentive to the unions to avoid a *calling in*, i.e. to settle at an earlier stage.

A complementary and compatible line of thought stems from the idea of a 'Public Representative', which fits in well with your own repeated emphasis on the rights of the consumer in these matters. If the unions or the employers want the help of professional conciliators, then that could automatically involve the participation of a 'Public Representative' who would be an integral part of whatever conciliation machinery was set up. If the dispute went beyond conciliation to arbitration then the 'Public Representative' would once again be involved. In short, the price which the parties would pay for conciliation would be inclusion of a 'Public Representative' in their conclaves.

These would be radical suggestions, and no doubt others could be thought of. But it would be hard to overestimate the political importance of getting this right. If the Government is firmly set against a statutory incomes policy, then it *must* have new techniques to make the old policy work. In 1972 the miners' strike and settlement were a setback. In 1973 a repetition would be a disaster. The worst course would be to continue on the present lines, hoping against the evidence that the present techniques are adequate.

The Prime Minister and his colleagues preferred to concentrate on a different approach. Despite some discussion on a CPRS paper they left untouched the relationship between the Government and the nationalized industries. They did not alter the techniques or habits of negotiation. They knew that in no circumstances could they sustain another defeat on the scale of February 1972. They set their minds to persuading the trade union leadership to accept a voluntary incomes policy. They were handicapped by the fury which the Industrial Relations Act had aroused – not of course among the public as a whole, nor among trade union members, but among the union leadership with whom Ministers had to deal. I do not know how close the talks in October 1972 between Government, trade unions, and employers came to success. Certainly the Prime Minister wore himself and others to the point of exhaustion in a most determined effort to reach agreement. A typical entry in my diary for 1 November: 'At Number Ten again till midnight while the endless tripartite talks go on – or rather don't go on, as it is almost all separate little huddles in every room and passage – including mine. EH hanging on still, against almost every calculation, to his hope of an agreement. Just a small chance he can wear them down.' It was a pattern which repeated itself a year later during the final dispute with the miners. We had a Prime Minister who believed passionately that realism should prevail if facts were reasonably presented. We had a Cabinet which, representing a modern Conservative Party, realized that in no way could that party prosper by setting class against class, however many warlike telegrams its supporters might send. Of all the charges now made against that Government, the charge that it sought or welcomed confrontation with the trade unions is the most absurd.

In the end the Prime Minister could not wear them down. On 6 November the Prime Minister announced in the House of Commons the decision to introduce a statutory incomes policy: it went well. Mr Wilson failed to create an occasion, Mr Powell hissed balefully from behind, and the Prime Minister easily survived. Ministers knew clearly the drawbacks and dangers of the new policy. Nevertheless, the long hours of talks produced one surprising effect. When we knew that there was no agreement we began sadly to think of contingency plans against immediate industrial trouble. Nothing happened. The policy was respected. For a year there was industrial peace and the wage explosion was averted. That is not of course an argument for a permanent incomes policy. It does show that an imposed statutory policy can be temporarily effective. I doubt if this would have been achieved if it had not been for the apparently abortive talks beforehand.

It remains true that a sense of realism on all sides is the only cure for such troubles. This is a platitude easier to state than achieve. With benefit of hindsight, it was unrealistic of the Government to impose the Industrial Relations Act. With benefit of hindsight, the trade union leaders were unrealistic to refuse a voluntary incomes policy in 1972, and to destroy a statutory policy fifteen months later. If they had acted otherwise, the standard of living of their members would almost certainly be substantially higher than it is today. Today adversity has dinned a lot more realism into all of us than existed in 1972. That fact offers the most solid ground for hope.

But there is perhaps something to add at a more mundane level. The relationship between Government and nationalized industries is still not right. There is still uneasy ambiguity in the handling of public sector disputes. I have mentioned the suggestion that, since the Government had the responsibility for the outcome of negotiations, it should take the power to conduct them. It should 'call in' a negotiation if it was of national importance, arranging for a Minister to carry it forward instead of the head of the nationalized body. The alternative is to resolve the ambiguity by moving in the opposite direction. The adoption of cash limits would increase the distance between the Minister and the nationalized industry. The management of the industry would be free to increase wages and salaries at will, provided only that it could finance them without coming back to the Government for more.

This approach was not seriously tried between 1970 and 1974. Those concerned were still under the influence of Lord Plowden's report on public spending, which emphasized the importance of measuring in terms of resources rather than of cash. A cash limit policy would, I suppose, have been dismissed as unrealistic. Certainly it, like any other policy, has its risks. Unless something were done to curb price increases imposed by state monopolies on goods or services which the citizen finds essential, a policy relying solely on cash limits could result in much higher prices in the public sector, for these monopolies would find that it was easier to put up prices than to resist excessive wage claims. Cash limits might not at first be credible, for management and trade unions would have to be persuaded that, when the crunch came, the Government really would refuse extra finance for a settlement outside the cash limits. It would lead to widely varied settlements within the public sector, which would in this respect become more like the private sector, where firms grant pay increases which vary according to their success. There would need to be clearly identified Government help for any services which Government expected nationalized industries to run against their commercial judgement. These changes would at first be unfamiliar, and therefore, since this is Britain, unpopular. Once they had been sustained past the first shocks, their wisdom might become clear.

More may be needed. During this troubled period many felt the need for an organization which did not exist – a union of consumers dedicated to oppose and resist strikes. We felt, indeed sometimes we knew, that public opinion was against those who inflicted inconvenience or hardship on the public – yet public opinion had no means of asserting itself. A political party is too narrow an instrument for this purpose. Since then Ministers have manned picket lines in an industrial dispute, so I suppose it will be in order in future for Ministers to break picket lines as well; but it seems unlikely to become a widespread habit. Unless public sector disputes subside into insignificance a counterforce will eventually be created. It may be ugly, or it may be sensible, but the public will not remain for ever content to suffer as innocent victim of disputes over which it has no control. The law and the habits of action governing the conduct of strikes were formed to cope with disputes in the private sector. These were a trial of strength between employer and the employee, each capable of inflicting real damage on the other. Now in a public sector dispute the employee barely suffers. Any temporary loss of income is usually covered by the union, and is in any case quickly recouped out of the eventual settlement. The employer, the actual administrator of the public concern, does not suffer at all, for his salary is secure. It is the public, and only the public, which suffers, first as consumer and later, when the bill comes in, as taxpayer. The public picks up the tab for both sides. It is a wholly absurd situation. Yet we carry on with rules and conventions which ignore this fact. It is a commonplace for trade union leaders to say 'we have no quarrel with the public' after they have closed schools, stopped trains, or paralysed airports. In fact it is *only* the public with which they are quarrelling. So far the public have lain down under this extraordinary double talk. Their patience has been amazing. Politicians and communicators consistently disguise what is happening by talking in the old terms of a trial of strength between employer and employee. One day people will wake up to their own interests, and the uninhibited right to strike against the public will begin to wither away in the heat of public reaction.

I have lingered over this question of public sector disputes because they were important, and in the end fatal. The Government's handling of some other parts of its economic policy was on the whole deft and intelligent. Because there were very few leaks from Cabinet and Ministerial meetings, Ministers were able to use the weapon of surprise. Mr Barber's budgets, the decision to float the pound, and the launching of each phase of the incomes policy were all tactically successful operations. Ministers got on well together. There seemed to be remarkably little bickering. Under the surface the confidence of the Parliamentary Party was gradually being eroded, but this was masked by Francis Pym's exceptional skill as Chief Whip. The Prime Minister and most of his colleagues were well liked by those who worked with them. The general atmosphere, even in moments of crisis, was genial. Personally, I believed that the Government would win through, not least because of the Prime Minister's particular brand of leadership.

On Sunday 18 March 1973, senior Ministers with a few advisers met at Chequers to discuss political strategy. 'PM v. genial and relaxed in yellow pullover, rest of us tweeds. Hazy sun and endless coffee in yellow and white parlour . . . Tour the half-finished swimming pool. Everyone calm and reasonably reflective over the two-year prospect. Prices should come right slowly after mid-1973, and unemployment come right too fast. Balance of payments will get worse, then better. If no horrors occur, Autumn 1974 might be best (for an election) . . . But we need to be more diligent in housing and more political in everything. [We are] in good with old, in bad with young.' 'If no horrors occur . . .' No one can predict world commodity prices, though in Britain even the most sceptical politicians have to try. Commodity prices had been rising at an alarming rate since 1972 but anyone who at that meeting in March 1973 had predicted a quadrupling of the price of oil within a year would have been laughed from the room.

The following week-end Mr Heath had a good press for speeches in Newcastle and at the Conservative College at Swinton. Another public sector dispute, in the gas industry, was crumbling. On Monday as usual the Liaison Committee met in the Lord President's room. Francis Pym, normally cautious to the point of gloom, remarked: 'I've never said it before, I'll probably never say it again – but the Government has had a fantastically good week.' So, though the problems multiplied, there were ups as well as downs.

The belief that all would come right for the Government in the end was strengthened by the eclipse of the Labour Party. Mr Harold Wilson was sometimes effective in debate, but much less often than before 1970. The role of Leader of the Opposition, which he had so relished in the early 1960s, seemed no longer to suit him. There was a bitter public dispute within the Labour Party about Europe during which Mr Roy Jenkins resigned as Deputy Leader. The Labour Party won the Bromsgrove by-election from the Government in 1971, but it never gained another seat before the General Election. Indeed it lost seats to the Liberals and Scottish Nationalists. The Labour Party was important in these years because of the encouragement which it gave to the trade unions to frustrate the Government's economic policy. As an alternative Government, it seemed unpopular and unconvincing. And it remained so: when final defeat came, it came not because Labour gained votes, but because we lost them.

Electorally our problem was with the Liberals. As in 1962 Conservative voters disappointed with the Government switched to Liberal in by-elections to record their protest. The scale of this switch was formidable. By the end no seat was safe. Indeed paradoxically the safer the seat had been, the more it was at risk. In the small hours of 8 December 1972, two by-election results were announced. The Government lost Sutton and Cheam catastrophically by 7000 but 20 minutes later hung on to Uxbridge. In a marginal seat like Uxbridge the challenge came from Labour. Our party organization there was in good trim, and constantly on the alert. They were used to a close result and knew how to fight. In the counties and the south coast resorts the story was different. Respected Members of Parliament died, a ruthless searchlight was turned on their constituencies and all was found not to be well. Some associations appeared to consist mainly of office holders. The notepaper looked fine, but there were no troops. Local Conservative Councils turned out to have been negligent or worse.

There was no time in a few weeks to retrieve the ground lost over the years. There appeared at once a Liberal candidate, difficult to attack because he stood for nothing, scurrying hither and thither in a blaze of publicity, pressing home a skilful assault. The more trivial the issue the greater the noise. In July 1973 there were campaigns in Ripon and Isle of Ely. Sir Malcolm Stoddart-Scott and Sir Henry Legge-Bourke had won impeccable majorities for many years. By then however we were in no doubt of the peril haunting the shires. Two days before polling day I reported to the Prime Minister on a meeting at Central Office.

By-Elections

RW [Richard Webster] reported today that the result was likely to be close in both. He felt that the atmosphere was similar to that in summer 1963, when everyone wanted to kick the Government. This time, however, there was just one issue, and that was prices.

In both seats the Liberals had come up from nowhere and were challenging hard, the Labour campaign having failed to get off the ground in Ripon, though the solid Labour agricultural worker vote in Ely might save them (and therefore us) from disaster.

The fighting fund appeals in each seat had been successful, but it was hard to find many local canvassers. This deficiency had been made good by outsiders, but it was not an encouraging symptom.

Both Ely and Ripon succumbed.

Within the Conservative Party one result quickly became

apparent. Indeed it has turned out to be the only permanent result of that particular Liberal revival. Members of Parliament and candidates became much more concerned with the minor details of life in their constituencies. This was the start of the revival of so-called community politics. Liberal candidates could be seen peering hopefully at leaky roofs of council houses. They weeded dandelions from cracked pavements. They asked old ladies whether it might suit them better if the bus-stop were moved a hundred yards down the road. No project in town or village was too small for their attention. They exaggerated, but they did us good. It was no longer enough for Members of Parliament to impress their colleagues or the national press with their knowledge of national problems. They had to be active and visible in local affairs; they had to know what was actually happening to their actual constituents. The healthy trend was already there. The Liberals gave the trend a jerk forward. Of course some MPs had always been 'good constituency members'; from now on it was unsafe to be anything else.

Community politics nevertheless played a smaller part in the Liberal gains than public discontent over prices. All kinds of explanation were given, but once again it was inflation that counted. In July 1973 Ministers were beginning to consider the form of Stage 3 of the incomes policy. The first two stages had held remarkably well, but the rise in world commodity prices had substituted one cause of inflation for another. The next stage would obviously have to be more flexible and allow some restoration of differentials.

CHAPTER EIGHT

INTO THE DARK

September is the best month for political campaigning. The weather is usually good, the days still long; people are back from their holidays, but Parliament is not sitting. The Prime Minister had been persuaded to carry out a series of political tours in September 1973. We had done this each year in opposition, but since 1970 the chores of government had got in the way. The disastrous results at Ely and Ripon showed that the Government had again fallen into a pit of unpopularity. I had hoped that by September there would be a more imaginative message to give about inflation, but this had been frustrated. Nevertheless, there was a great deal to be said for the Government which was not being said often or clearly enough. Both Mr Heath and the Conservative Party stood to benefit if he snatched seven or eight days out of one month and spent them on the stump outside London. He approved the plan of meetings at the beginning of August, on the understanding, which I put to him in a minute, that 'It is not the purpose of the programme that you should announce new policies or take new initiatives'.

On Sunday 2 September we sat in the sun on the terrace at Chequers eating scones and tarts while my small sons splashed in the new swimming pool. As usual it was difficult to pin down the conversation. Mr Heath talked about the Commonwealth Conference at Ottawa, about Ulster, about possible Ministerial changes. It was clear that he would have no real holiday that summer. But we also managed to discuss the coming tours. 'PM now prepared to give much more energy to political matters – but not prepared to change his essential concentration on what he thinks important e.g. Ireland, Europe, even though political gains are obscure.' Two days later we set off on the first visit, to his own county of Kent. Then to Dunfermline and East Lothian. At Port Seton at lunchtime there was a ludicrous mishap. The Scots had been asked to arrange a meeting of local businessmen, but when we arrived the audience consisted almost entirely of old ladies. They endured philosophically and with only slight puzzlement a heavy speech of economic analysis which had already been released to the press. Somewhere along the line there had been a lapse. I tried not very successfully to persuade the Prime Minister that in Scotland because of their academic tradition old ladies expected solid fare. He was soothed by Peter Pears singing *Death in Venice* at the Edinburgh Festival that evening.

Some of the flavour of these expeditions emerges from my diary for the following week. '14 September. A hot sunny day election-eering in Walsall, for reasons which in retrospect are by no means clear. Garden room girl extensively sick in helicopter. Hours 9.30–11.30 spent quickly and strenuously putting speech in order. Day overshadowed by building societies bashing up the rate to 11% despite Barber's concessions. Otherwise v. successful. At lunch in the Town Hall he delivers heavyish stuff very clearly and well – as he becomes accustomed to electioneering again he gets better at it. A primary school – he conducts a calypso – knots of waving women in sunny streets – a hospital – walk down the main street in a big cheerful crowd – local editors and gin – party workers and back to tea – another clear quiet speech. Away by 7.30.'

The next day at the Newbury Show 'a good friendly crowd apart from a tense mad tent of anti-Marketeers', then to a big rally at Stratfield Saye where he was mobbed by autograph hunters, finally a meeting at a private house near Reading. The following week to Newcastle, the week after that a day with six meetings in Hertfordshire and Essex. His reception was markedly friendly. That indeed was the main message from these excursions. No one in the autumn of 1973 was thinking of an early election. The aim was to keep the political race sufficiently open to leave the Prime Minister a choice of dates later on. We could not afford to fall hopelessly behind in the polls. On 3 October, I put in the black box at Number Ten an opinion poll to be published the next day: 'Labour 34, Liberal 32, Conservative 31. I asked Central Office to check and they find a similar position in March 1962, except that Liberals were then narrowly ahead of Labour.' This was indeed an open race, outwardly bad for us, but paradoxically full of hope. For it was reasonable to guess that, as had happened before, the Liberal vote was swollen by Conservative dissidents who would return to us in a general election. Against this background we knew from the tours and the reception which he received that Mr Heath remained a formidable and respected campaigner.

In view of much that has been written since, one incident is worth mentioning. Mr Heath's speeches during these September tours, as we have seen, were not designed to break new ground. He expounded the growth policy and the success of Stage 2 on familiar lines. Near the beginning I was asked to go round to the Treasury to see the Chancellor of the Exchequer. I understood that he was worried by a phrase in the Prime Minister's speech the day before. There was always a difficulty in clearing speeches with Ministers when so many were being made in a short space of time, but that was no excuse. In the nicest possible way Mr Barber went over the ground with me and ensured that references to future economic expansion must be carefully related to productive capacity. The idea that right up to the Yom Kippur war Ministers were galloping ahead with wild ideas of expansion unrelated to capacity is not correct. There were errors of rhetoric, but the need to slow down was already recognized.

On Sunday 7 October Mr Heath held a working dinner at Chequers. Because historians tend to analyse one subject at a time they sometimes lose sight of the pell-mell of politics. Problems crowd in on top of each other, competing for scarce time. The immediate topic often crowds out something more important. The principal actors thrive for a time on the excitement of this way of life. They do not notice the onset of fatigue. But if they allow themselves no respite their pace slows, they increasingly miss their stroke, they begin without realizing it to move through a fog of tiredness. This happened to Ministers in the winter of 1973. Perhaps the first signs were apparent on that Sunday evening, though I did not spot them. Certainly the events were already crowding in. There had been a visit from Chancellor Brandt of West Germany. There had been a ragged and difficult set of decisions to take on Stage 3 of the incomes policy, to be announced by the Prime Minister the next day. Ministers had been for some days at odds, and almost for the first time news of their dissensions had spread widely in Whitehall. Also unsettling was the prospect of Ministerial changes which were known to be in the offing, but not yet decided. The annual Party Conference was imminent and bound to be difficult. And on top of all, reducing everything else to insignificance, Israelis and Arabs were yet again fighting each other in the Middle East.

Not that we all understood as early as this the disaster which the Yom Kippur war would bring on us. Indeed that Sunday I was peevish because the Prime Minister spent so much time thinking and talking about it. I fumed when I learned that Sheikh Zaid, the ruler of Abu Dhabi, was coming down to Chequers at once. Rulers from the Gulf were not men to be bowed in and out in ten minutes or half an hour. They required coffee and much ceremonious chat. A large slice of precious time would be thrown away on a matter which, however fascinating, the Prime Minister could hardly hope to influence. Far better to concentrate on the business in hand, the statement on Stage 3 of the incomes policy to be made at Lancaster House the next afternoon, and the Party Conference with Mr Heath's own vital speech only six days away and still unprepared. The hours were ticking away, there was so much to be done, no one was doing it. The feeling of frustrated impatience was by then very familiar. As a former member of the Foreign Service I should have known better. The Party Conference, even Stage 3, were to be much less important to Britain in coming months than the decisions of Sheikh Zaid and his fellow oil-producers.

The news of the war overshadowed the announcement of Stage 3, which was perhaps just as well. Mr Heath allowed himself to become too technical. Much of his matter was incomprehensible to the journalists at the press conference, let alone the television audience that evening. The Party Conference on the other hand went well. There was no sense of impending doom. The dangerous debates passed off quietly. The Prime Minister as usual went to an endless round of parties, and still on Thursday work on the Conference speech for Saturday had hardly begun.

In the end all went well, and as usual there was a family lunch after the speech. This was the sixth that I attended and the last that Mr Heath held. We travelled back to London by plane. During the flight, to the despair of civil servants with full red boxes, the Prime Minister, the Foreign Secretary and the Chancellor of the Exchequer all slept soundly.

During November 1973 the earth began to move under the Government's feet. Our oil supplies were going to be cut by the producers. There was an immense confusion of information and much hectic diplomacy, so no one could yet tell how harshly we would actually have to cut our consumption. At the same time the Government was being drawn into a struggle with the miners on incomes policy. The Conservative Party, its Leader, its Ministers, its backbenchers and its supporters in the country had already been beaten on this very ground in 1972. We had most of us dreaded, beyond anything else, a further engagement with the miners. Yet here we were being manoeuvred once again towards the same fatal field, still littered with relics of the last defeat.

But of course while these dangers gathered, ordinary political life went on. People do not stop doing small things because big events are impending. On 24 October the Prime Minister for the first time took part in a BBC phone-in programme. This was an idea put forward by Don Harker, the Director of Publicity at Central Office. I had strongly backed it on the simple ground that Mr Heath was usually better at answering questions than at making pronouncements. The broadcast went well. The same evening Princess Margaret dined at Number Ten with Duke Ellington. We had to extricate the Prime Minister from the meal to hear Sir Alec Douglas-Home's account of a sudden new crisis which, according to Dr Kissinger, had blown up in the Middle East. The next day the Government reshuffle, pending for so long, was once again postponed because Mr Whitelaw needed a week or two more in Northern Ireland. That morning the Chief Whip was very gloomy about a vote in the Commons on the Channel Tunnel, but when the vote came in the evening there was a Government majority of sixty. And so on and so on. Each day had for Ministers its sequence of anxieties, of unexpected news, of urgent decisions on a range of unrelated matters. At the heart of a real crisis for a few days this sequence is interrupted while everyone concentrates briefly on the central issue. But this interruption can only be temporary, otherwise the whole process of government will come to a halt. In November they had not yet reached that stage.

Central Office was preoccupied with the four by-elections which were held on 8 November. We were defending three seats, two against a Liberal challenge, one against Labour. It is worth recalling how pitiful the Labour showing was, even though they were only four months away from a partial General Election victory. They totally failed to shake our seat in Edinburgh North, and they actually lost a seat of their own in Glasgow to the Scottish Nationalists. Interest centred on the Liberal attack at Berwick and at Hove. On their showing in July the Liberals should have gathered Berwick without difficulty. But we had a good candidate and, for once, a good local organization. It was clearly going to be close.

Hove should have been impregnable, but to almost everyone who went there it felt wrong. The local organization had mouldered away, the Conservative Council had been much criticized, and though we had a good candidate he faced a tough opponent with a flair for headlines. There was a real worry that we would lose, and that the resulting panic would get out of hand. It had become a ritual of by-elections that Sir Richard Webster, the Director of Organization at Central Office, should chance his arm with a private prediction to the Central Office Tactical Committee. On 6 November 'RW's answer is that we lose Berwick, keep Hove and Edinburgh, and the SNP may snatch Govan. Not bad if true.' And so exactly it turned out two days later. It was sad to lose Berwick by a handful of votes. However, the Liberal assault which had been unstoppable in July had received its first check, and the Labour Party looked distinctly sick. The opinion polls told, though less clearly, a similar story. That was the electoral background to the decisions which the Prime Minister soon had to face.

The progress of discussions with the miners showed how little had been learned about the tactical handling of public sector disputes. Once again the crucial opening rounds were in the hands of the nationalized board. Once again the board decided to give away everything at once. (In this case the National Coal Board's offer included not only the biggest basic increase allowed under the incomes policy, but also an amount for the 'unsocial hours' worked by many miners – a concept which had been built into the incomes policy in an attempt to ease precisely this hard case). Once again the National Union of Mineworkers, accustomed to negotiate, rejected this first offer as wholly inadequate. Once again the trade union was tireless in putting its case to the public. On 12 November I minuted to the Prime Minister under the heading 'Miners – publicity': 'The Party (and Jim Prior) are still deeply worried about this. The press is good. But on radio/TV the NUM have it mostly their own way.' I went on to make rude remarks about the information side of the Department of Trade and Industry.

On 8 November the NUM Executive voted for an overtime ban. Five days later the Government, determined to avoid the delays which had done harm in 1972, declared a state of emergency, and introduced regulations to cut the use of electricity.

One odd thing about the weeks which followed was that every now and then by some silent agreement everyone forgot the crisis for a few days and thought of something else. This happened for Princess Anne's wedding in mid-November. 'A fine brisk day for the wedding, and all goes splendidly. Nip out to the Horse Guards to watch them drive back. Leaves and breastplates and a smiling Queen. After all the carping the magic works.' Then immediately there was a meeting about the need for a Ministerial broadcast.

By the middle of the month it was becoming clear that things were badly wrong. The oil crisis and the coal crisis could not be kept distinct. Together they were shaking the whole strategy of economic expansion. This had become more cautious in September before either crisis had occurred. Now, under the impact of the double crisis, it would have to be reversed. Exactly when and exactly how had still to be settled.

As happens on such occasions Ministers were discussing among themselves measures which it would have been wrong even to mention to Party officials. Liaison became more difficult. The political advisers in Whitehall knew more than those at Central Office, much less than Ministers. Ministers, by now tiring and always in a hurry, were less ready to spend the odd five minutes in informal chat. The political advisers drew together to pool our information and clear our thoughts. From now on we met often in my office at Number Ten.

Under an immense work load the Prime Minister remained calm and unfussed. He was kept going by his own gifts of humour and courage. He held to a plan to tour north-east Lancashire on 22 and 23 November. As usual this expedition out of London went reasonably well, and the contact with real life lifted his spirits. On the way back we had a long talk of a kind which was becoming increasingly difficult in London because of the pressures of time. I suggested that someone somewhere should be charting all the possible courses of the coal dispute. Although the Government had acted early and well to conserve stocks, it was hard to see the way through to a tolerable ending. Mr Heath was more concerned about oil. He felt that the Foreign Office might not be exerting its full diplomatic strength to safeguard supplies.

On 27 November a meeting was called at Number Ten to brief the Prime Minister for his meeting with the Miners' Executive the next day. It should have provided a chance for that clear-headed analysis of the options before the Government, which was by then badly needed. Instead there was silence on the big issues and a confused, bitty discussion of trivial tactical points. I felt critical of the senior civil servants present, whose duty it should have been to force the discussion into some coherent channel. This was the third and final occasion when I felt that at a crucial moment they fell below what was required. The others had occurred after Bloody Sunday in Londonderry in 1972, and during the discussion of inflation in the summer of 1973. No one who was present at any of these three meetings could believe that the civil service runs this country.

That week-end I went to the Christmas supper organized by the Forest Hill branch of the Mid-Oxfordshire Conservative Association. Forest Hill is a small village on the ridge above Oxford, and its Christmas supper is traditional and splendid. Because of the petrol shortage garages along the road were dark and shut. Perhaps impressed by this experience, I gave them after the turkey a short speech of unexampled gloom. Everything was going wrong. The prospect had never been darker. Great sacrifice would be required by all. This went extremely well, and seemed to cheer them immensely. Their reaction strengthened a feeling which was already growing in my mind.

On 6 December the political advisers met informally to review the situation. About this time we were much strengthened by the arrival in the Political Office at Number Ten of William Waldegrave, who crossed into these stormier waters from the comparative calm of the Central Policy Review Staff. We drafted a paper for the Prime Minister which I sent to him that night under a covering note. In this note I tried to set out the case for putting a gloomy face on the situation:

Up till now the Government has concentrated on treating each problem on its merits, trying to preserve business confidence and continuing to speak about sustained expansion. The particular aspect of this policy which has caught public attention is the refusal to announce petrol rationing.

In our view this general policy, though there were strong reasons for it, has now reached the end of its possibilities. In view of events across the world it is not any longer credible to speak of any *substantial* growth in the British economy during 1974, as NEDO recognized yesterday. Business confidence has been temporarily crushed. In the particular case of petrol there is widespread demand for rationing (80% in favour according to Harris today). If the Government were to continue through December with its present general approach it would increasingly be felt to be out of touch with reality and to have lost its grip on events. What is already true in the case of petrol could quickly become true also in the more important fields of industrial unrest and the general economic situation.

Apparent loss of grip would do more political damage to the Government than any measures, however unpopular.

There is therefore, in our view, a strong argument for a change of approach over the next 7/8 days. The Government should seek to *emphasize* the gravity of the situation, drawing together the various threads. Next week is particularly important because of the NUM meeting on the 13th, and the possible start of action on the railways which would gravely inconvenience individuals and give a further serious twist to the energy situation.

One disadvantage of this change of course would be the need to explain fairly optimistic statements made by ministers until fairly recently. We believe that this difficulty can be overcome. The opportunities which ministers were describing *did exist*, but have been temporarily buried by the landslide of world events and industrial unrest. The Government's job is to clear away this debris and recreate the opportunities.

The main advantage of the change of approach would be that it would enable the Government to justify measures which in more normal terms would be impossible. We are thinking in particular in terms of a Treasury package. The new atmosphere would make it more likely to achieve a tolerable settlement of industrial disputes. By restoring the political authority of the Government it would pave the way for an early General Election, if you decided that this was desirable.

The main paper agreed by the political advisers looked at the possibility that the coal dispute would drag on after Christmas. We recorded our view that 'a settlement in manifest breach of Stage 3 would not be possible for this Government, because it would destroy its authority and break the morale of the Conservative Party beyond hope of restoration in the lifetime of this Parliament'. In retrospect I hold to that.

We went on to consider the economic measures which the Government might then have to take. Finally we looked cautiously at the idea of an early General Election. The drafting here shows signs of more than one view, but it was prophetic.

The practical difficulties of holding an Election in these circumstances would be great, but doubtless they could be overcome. It would be a highly charged and violent Election, and it would of course be impossible to confine it to any one issue. The Government's election campaign would only be credible if it included proposals which would bring an end to the industrial action. It is not easy to see what these would be. A situation in which the NUM could influence the result of an Election by saying they would return to work if Labour were elected would clearly be dangerous. There is an important distinction between an early election held in the middle of an industrial crisis, and an early election held soon after the immediate crisis had passed. For the reasons just given the latter would be greatly preferable.

The general arguments for an Election fairly early next year are becoming very strong. In particular:

a) The important economic indicators are not likely to improve in time to have a political impact in the lifetime of this Parliament.
b) Both the Opposition Parties are now in trouble, but will make strenuous efforts to get out of it during 1974. The timing of the South Worcestershire by-election is important in this respect.
c) The authority of government will gradually diminish during 1974 as the natural end of the Parliament approaches. This is particularly important in the context of Stage 3, or its successor.

It would be wrong in these circumstances to take any action now which would make an early election impossible. We need to work quietly but fast on the additional themes which would be required to fight such an election, e.g. on industrial relations and on the conservation of energy as a long-term policy.

I have quoted at some length from this paper, not because it was in itself particularly important, but because it shows some of the ideas and arguments then current. The Prime Minister read it promptly and, as was his custom, returned it to me politely with a 'Thank you' scribbled at the top.

As will already have been seen there was much talk at this time about petrol rationing; indeed coupons were actually issued. Those of us who wanted the Government to underline at every turn the gravity of the double crisis feared that petrol rationing would be inevitable in the end, but might be delayed for political reasons which we felt were out-of-date. The Prime Minister, backed by Peter Walker, who at this stage was still responsible for energy, resisted this advice. They pointed out that petrol rationing in 1973 would be a different proposition from the rationing which had worked quite well in 1956–7 at the time of Suez. Many more people now relied on cars, particularly in country districts, and the complications of administering different exemptions and allowances would be almost intolerable. This view turned out to be entirely correct. If it had not been for the overshadowing coal dispute, the Government's handling of the physical oil shortage would have been recognized as skilful, after some early confusion. There was nothing which they could do to avert the quadrupling of the oil price, which turned out to be infinitely more harmful than the physical shortage.

In December the coal dispute dragged on unsatisfactorily. Mr Whitelaw was at last brought back from Ulster to take over the Department of Employment. The deadlock in discussions with the miners was unbroken. A rush of other events prevented senior Ministers from giving the coal crisis the attention which it needed.

On Sunday 8 December, for example, the Prime Minister entertained the Italian Prime Minister, Signor Rumor, to dinner at Chequers. The meal was hardly over when Mr Heath flew to Sunningdale by helicopter to preside over the last stage of the conference on the future of Northern Ireland. Three days later it was time for the State Visit of President Mobutu of Zaire. Two days after that the European summit began in Copenhagen. These were four major events, two of them (Sunningdale and Copenhagen) of outstanding importance. They were all the kind of diplomatic event which in normal times Mr Heath would much enjoy and at which he would perform very well. They all involved talks, travel, long meals, extensive briefing beforehand; yet none of them had anything to do with the crisis which was swallowing us up.

By 11 December the Conservative Party was at its senior levels much alarmed. That morning at the Tactical Committee I was told that it was essential that the Prime Minister should broadcast without delay. There was no very clear notion as to what he should say; but that he should say something was evident to all. The next day Lord Carrington, as Chairman of the Party, forcefully supported this advice. At these discussions I was doubtful because I knew that Mr Heath disliked broadcasting when he had nothing positive to say. I also knew that although he might be persuaded to broadcast, a Prime Ministerial broadcast which the Prime Minister himself at heart disliked was not likely to be a great success. A broadcast should be used to reinforce action, not as a substitute for it. However, later in the week the three day week was announced and Ministers reached agreement on an economic package including drastic expenditure cuts. The broadcast was made on 13 December. It came over reasonably well, but there had been, as usual, too many hands at work on the text. This had been snatched from Michael Wolff and myself by Sir William Armstrong, and snatched back again by us a few hours before delivery. The hour that afternoon which the Prime Minister should have spent putting his personal imprint on what he was going to say was spent instead ironing out a last-minute difficulty which had cropped up over the creation of a new Department of Energy.

During this period speculation about an early election began to mount. At this stage it was only speculation. Nigel Lawson had been asked to draft a manifesto which might be used in a crisis election. We all noted an opinion poll on 7 December which put the Conservatives five points ahead. But there was at this stage, so far as I know, no serious discussion of an early election among senior Ministers. Certainly the Prime Minister had not yet begun to address his mind to the idea. Those of us who knew his natural caution understood that he would take a lot of persuading. The decision to introduce a three day week was not influenced by any thought of an election. On 18 December 'Slowly the band waggon for an early General Election is beginning to roll – but EH, so far as one can gather, still unconvinced'.

Christmas provided another interlude, this time a long one. I spent six days in Oxfordshire and do not recall that the Prime Minister telephoned once – an experience unique, I think, in the six years that I worked for him. Because of the timely introduction of the three day week there was no prospect of an early national breakdown. The miners were still operating an overtime ban, not a strike. There was therefore some time in hand, but no coherent plan for using it. The Government had so far resisted various compromise suggestions which would have amounted to a breach of Stage 3. In this they were strongly sustained by the Conservative Party in the country. But this stand had no future unless a new element was introduced into the situation. That element, so far lacking, was a means of pressure on the miners to suspend their action and accept something not too far ahead of the privileged position which was already assured them under the 'unsocial hours' clauses of Stage 3. A plain man could think of several ways of introducing this element of pressure, for example by withdrawing the original NCB offer, by linking more clearly the future financing of the industry by the taxpayer to reasonable co-operation from the miners, or by ordering a ballot under the Industrial Relations Act. All those concerned with the industry were sure that any such plain action would be counter-productive, exacerbate the situation, and so forth.

On Friday 28 December I went back to Downing Street. There was a considerable commotion about payment for the time which coal miners spend in the baths. A few people suggested that if the

Pay Board took a more generous view of this, the extra money involved might be enough to break the deadlock. On examination the idea was too flimsy to work. There was more rather aimless talk that day of an early election, and indeed of a new total freeze on pay and prices.

Whatever happened in the rest of the country there would have to be an election in South Worcestershire, because of the recent death of Sir Gerald Nabarro. A by-election there would of course test again the Government's ability to hold so-called safe seats against the Liberals. It would also test the public view of the miners' overtime ban and the three day week. South Worcestershire did not loom large in many people's minds, but it had to in mine. There was a convention, now abandoned by Mrs Thatcher, that the Leader of the Conservative Party did not campaign in by-elections. Mr Heath decided that in spite of this he would go to Worcestershire and talk to Party supporters before the campaign began.

New Year's Eve, the date fixed for this visit, was a splendid winter's day of mist, sun and frost. That afternoon I stood with a group of dignitaries waiting for the Prime Minister by the bridge at Upton-on-Severn. Michael Spicer, the Conservative candidate and the officers of the South Worcestershire Association had the patient professional air of regimental officers awaiting briefing from their Commander in Chief on the eve of a particularly desperate battle. The sun declined, the mist on the Severn meadows thickened, the frost began to bite through our coats. The Prime Minister was late, not an unknown occurrence, though this time there was a reason. At last he arrived, almost too late to be photographed in daylight with Michael Spicer, and walked up the hill to the meeting hall past small enthusiastic groups of people. In the hall he gave the Party workers a calm careful account of what had happened, and why we now had a three day week. It was in one way a remarkable occasion. Any other politician I have known would have seized and used the emotion hanging in the air. The country was tense, a struggle had begun on which our future seemed to rest. Here in this small market town the Prime Minister was talking to his supporters at the start of a crucial by-election. He had led them to unexpected victory in 1970, his courage and doggedness were immensely respected. He could have worked that audience to a pitch of fiery loyalty. He could have whipped them up against the miners. He could have sent them excited and enthusiastic into the streets. It did not occur to him to do so. What mattered to him was that they should understand the complexities of the issue, the objective facts and figures. He saw it as his duty to educate and inform, not to inflame one part of the country against another. So in one sense the meeting was a missed opportunity; but to those who wished to notice (a dwindling minority) it showed a Prime Minister who wanted to tackle not the miners, but inflation, the balance of payments and the desperate consequences for Britain of the oil crisis.

Personally I heard little of this. I was fussing to and fro between the hall and a tiny office with a telephone. It emerged that the Prime Minister had been late mainly because of a crisis in Ulster. The German Consul, Herr Niedermeyer, had been kidnapped, presumably by the IRA. The German Government had some information about the background to this, and was showing alarm. While the Prime Minister was speaking at Upton, word arrived that the German Ambassador in London had an urgent personal message from Chancellor Brandt which he was instructed to deliver to Mr Heath that night.

I had a personal interest in this, for it happened that Mr Heath had said he would dine at our house in Oxfordshire that evening before returning to Chequers. It seemed clear to me that this plan would now founder. Outside the mist was becoming fog. The Prime Minister had as usual an immense work load. If he consulted his own convenience, and that of the Ambassador, he would go straight back to Chequers and receive the German message there. The private secretary on duty obviously thought this would be sensible. I rang my wife to warn her that almost certainly her preparations would be wasted.

When Mr Heath emerged from answering questions he had quite other ideas. He had agreed to dine with us, people had been asked to meet him, dine with us he would. While I hurried home to pave the way, long and complicated instructions were telephoned to the German Embassy on the best means of finding the village of Alvescot in which we lived. We sent our small sons out on to the main road with lanterns and they waved in both Prime Minister and Ambassador through the freezing fog. In our dining-room, by candlelight, the poor travel-worn Ambassador handed over Herr Brandt's message, and the two men had a brisk argument about the delay in setting up the European Regional Fund. Later Mr Heath was in admirable form over our mushroom soup and beef, and left for Chequers half an hour before

the bells rang in 1974. For him it was not to be a Happy New
Year.

During the next five weeks, from 2 January until 7 February,
only two topics were of any interest in the Political Office at
Number Ten. Would we have an early election? If we did, how
could we win it? This was a decision which, under our conventions,
falls to be taken by the Prime Minister, not by Parliament or by
the Cabinet. The choice of an election date is one of the two
powers which make a British Prime Minister more than a chairman of his Cabinet colleagues, the other of course being the
power to choose those colleagues. But a Prime Minister in Mr
Heath's situation takes advice. Never, I suspect, has so much
advice been sought and given on the choice of an election date
as in those first five weeks of 1974. Cabinet colleagues expressed
their views. The division of opinion in the Parliamentary Party
was reported on many occasions by the new Chief Whip, Humphrey
Atkins. Lord Carrington and Mr Jim Prior had a particular
responsibility for giving advice as Chairman and Deputy Chairman
of the Party. The team of outside help which had contributed to
victory in 1970 put in their six-penny worth. Last and least, the
political advisers were far from silent. The Prime Minister
listened patiently at meeting after meeting. No less patiently he
read memorandum after memorandum. If he was exasperated
that so much of the advice was contradictory, he gave no sign.
Sometimes he conveyed one impression of his own views, sometimes another. Because those who produced this torrent of advice
knew him well, they did not regard this as vacillation. They knew
that as a cautious man he needed time to make up his mind.
They also knew that whatever the Party interest it would not in
the end be wholly or even mainly on party grounds that Mr Heath
would make the decision.

In the early days of January those who argued for an early
election were not necessarily thinking of February. A new
register of voters would come into force on 16 February. Because
of the greater efficiency of the Conservative organization in
gleaning postal votes from people who had moved house, there
would be a technical advantage in holding an election before
then on the old register. We thought this would be outweighed
by the feeling that to do so would be stealing an unfair advantage.
We would be presenting the Labour Party with a good argument
for questioning the whole basis of the election. When I discussed
dates on 7 January with Richard Webster at Central Office, we

talked in terms of 7 or 14 March. Fairly soon after that however, the horizon contracted. As events gathered pace those, including myself, who favoured an early election began to think in terms of polling day on 7 February.

On 6 January Mr Heath held a meeting of senior colleagues. I wrote that evening 'Hard to think of a PM who has such a decent likeable sane loyal core of colleagues'. The opinions expressed varied widely. Mr Heath had dinner with some of us at Pruniers that evening and said that it was exciting to feel an election in the air. I took that as a simple statement of fact, not as a sign that he had made up his mind.

On 9 January the TUC Economic Committee suggested that unions other than the NUM should undertake not to use any coal settlement in excess of the Stage 3 limits as an argument for breaking the incomes policy themselves. This struck and still strikes me as a flimsy proposal. There was a good deal of private evidence that the TUC would not in fact be able to hold back individual unions once the miners breached the policy. Nevertheless, the Prime Minister and Mr Whitelaw rightly considered that the TUC offer had to be explored, and this was done at a meeting at Number Ten on Thursday 10 January. As Political Secretary I had no standing to attend the meeting, but I hung about outside in the ante-room. When I learned that the meeting had been inconclusive and was to resume on Monday, I was much dismayed and showed it. The Prime Minister, emerging from the Cabinet Room, demanded that I explain my black looks. He was always quick to spot disapproval. I said that the issues were getting blurred, that an election would probably be needed, that it could only succeed if the Government could keep its stand against inflation clear-cut.

On Friday the Prime Minister went over the ground again with Lord Carrington, Jim Prior and Humphrey Atkins. He agreed at least that preparations should go ahead in case an early election was needed. That afternoon Mr Humphrey Taylor of the Opinion Research Centre presented the latest private public opinion surveys at Central Office. ORC, and Humphrey Taylor in particular, had a strong hold on our judgements because they alone had predicted victory in 1970. The evidence of his surveys was not conclusive, but Humphrey Taylor in his exposition deduced that we should win an early election.

The next day, Saturday 12 January, was the turn of the 'outside help', the team which had advised Mr Heath in 1970 and from time to time thereafter. They dined at Chequers, drawn there from many places and professions by personal loyalty. Without concerting beforehand they all pressed for an early election. For the first time in my diary that night I drew a parallel which often occurred to me in the next few weeks – that of Queen Elizabeth fencing with her advisers over the decision to execute Mary Queen of Scots. The advisers argued cogently for execution; the Queen's instinct was the other way. She led them a pretty dance before the deed was done.

The following day, Sunday 13 January, the debate started all over again with different participants. The Steering Committee of the Party met at Chequers in the evening to review election preparations. This Committee, a body which was normally comatose, sprang to life at the prospect of an election. It consisted of senior members of the Cabinet and senior Party officials. As they went over the familiar arguments from a party point of view it became fairly clear that the practical difficulties of fighting an election on 7 February would be enormous. The Party officials departed about 10.30 p.m. but the Ministers stayed talking and drinking in the Long Gallery upstairs for an hour or so more. The discussion became diffuse and wandering. 'Unhappy evening. We are in a desperate plight. I long to get the election behind us.'

There were three more days of intense argument. The renewed meeting with the TUC on Monday ended in deadlock, so the Prime Minister's hands were again free. 'Characteristically he refuses to show how he will use this freedom, but he is much more alert and cheerful after this marathon than he was yesterday, and I feel more hopeful of an early election. It is not certain of course, but other ways are blocked.'

On Tuesday the Steering Committee met again, this time in the Cabinet Room, in an attempt to complete the key passages in the manifesto which would be necessary if an election was called. No doubt deliberately the Prime Minister was slack in the chair, and we made slow progress. That evening there was a further Ministerial meeting, and in different forms the discussion continued through Wednesday and Thursday until all were exhausted. By Thursday evening, 17 January, the battle for an election on 7 February was lost. There was no more time. Suddenly the controversy stopped. Those who had argued most strongly for that date threw in the sponge. Nothing was settled except that this option was ruled out.

It is worth briefly stating the arguments. Though it cannot be proved I believe we would have won an election on 7 February. It would have taken place against the background of an overtime ban, not a strike. The three weeks which we lost brought with them, as we predicted, a steady ebb of the Government's authority. The issues became blurred. Practical people began to long for a settlement which would put the lights on again and get the factories back to a full working week. The dangers of inflation began to seem less important. The Government found the initiative slipping from its hand. The Opposition Parties had precious time to prepare themselves.

On 15 January I wrote a manuscript note to Mr Heath setting out part of the case for an early election. It is perhaps worth reproducing some of it to show where in my mind the balance of argument then lay:

> The aim of the Govt is a settlement which is not in manifest breach of Stage 3. The NUM have shown repeatedly that they cannot be persuaded into such a settlement. The Government's difficulty is that, failing *persuasion*, it has so far not managed to bring any kind of effective *pressure* to bear on the NUM. Effective pressure *has* been brought to bear on the TUC, with remarkable results; but I have heard no sensible person argue that in the absence of other pressures on the NUM the TUC could bring the NUM to accept a settlement as defined above.
>
> The danger of the last few weeks is that Ministers spend their time and ingenuity in most exhausting efforts to deal with particular tactical situations. These are difficult to handle. However successfully they are handled they do not bring us any nearer to a settlement as defined above; and meanwhile the stocks of coal diminish. We are gradually getting nearer the time when the Govt will be forced, by a revolution of business and public opinion and by the damage done to the nation, to accept a settlement clearly and substantially outside Stage 3.
>
> Private opinions differ as to whether this is an inevitable or tolerable outcome. After
>
> a) the experience of 1972:
> b) the frequent and specific pledges in recent weeks:
> c) the hardship to which people have been exposed as a result of the Government's stand.
>
> I suppose that such a settlement would provoke in the Party and outside a violent sense of betrayal, directed personally at you, and the Government would be brokenbacked for the remainder of its time.
>
> If this analysis is right, then it must be urgently necessary to bring

pressures to bear on the NUM. I have the impression that your senior advisers have despaired of this, because they operate within rather narrow parameters.

Disciplinary action in the pits, and a ballot under the IR Act, have been ruled out as too likely to produce a strike; and it is hard to argue sensibly against this judgement. We are left with:

a) *time*, i.e. in March the miners will at last be out of pocket because they will not be pocketing the extra money of the NCB offer. But this is a long time to wait. And is it a real pressure? The NCB will presumably backdate the extra pay to 1 March, so the loss to the miners will not be permanent. In any case it is only *extra* money which is involved. Time works more strongly *against* us.

b) the threat of a more stringent *Stage 4*, providing an incentive to settle under Stage 3. This was discussed briefly in Steering Committee today.

c) *an election* which if the Conservatives won, would create a new situation – both because the miners would face a Government armed with fresh authority and because the Government would have a much freer hand.

This is a desperately difficult decision. Advice is conflicting. So is the research on public opinion. It is very far from the sort of election which you or any sane Conservative would actually want to fight. The risks are very great.

The result of the election would depend on whether the deep dislike of trade union militancy which the research reveals (and which I personally think is the deepest instinct at present in our public opinion) is stronger than the unpopularity of the Government. I agree with Humphrey Taylor et al that it is stronger at present, but will not remain so. It was probably inevitable to reject 7 February, but 14 February is a different matter. A decision to reject 14 February would in practice involve a decision that in autumn 1974 or spring 1975 we would be better placed. Given the economic situation, and the political consequences of a coal settlement substantially outside Stage 3, this is not easy to sustain.

It is worth noting that no one in a position to give advice believed that the Conservatives would be bound to win an election. Nor did we believe that an election could or should be confined to the single issue of 'who governs?' On the contrary, part of the argument for an early election was that the Government needed a chance to discuss the charged economic situation with the electorate, and gain a new mandate for harsh measures. Nor did we believe or argue that an election victory would automatically solve the coal dispute. Mr Enoch Powell in a baleful comment accused the Party of dishonesty in making this pretence; he was wide of the mark. Obviously the miners would continue to press their case; but they would be faced with a Government with five years authority ahead of it, in particular with authority over the future of the coal industry. At present the Government held a desperately weak hand. No one was proposing any alternative way of strengthening it. An election victory would give the Government strong new cards. It certainly needed them.

Mr Heath, backed by two or three of his wisest colleagues, looked more widely and came to a different view. First of all they saw what was at stake. We faced an Opposition under appalling leadership. Mr Wilson appeared at this time to have no convictions of any kind. There was no point at which he could be relied on to resist the onset within the Labour Party of their peculiar and destructive blend of chauvinist Marxism. Our membership of the EEC was clearly at risk. So was the fragile Irish settlement so painfully put together at Sunningdale. So were the prospects for the private sector of British industry in the aftermath of the oil crisis. The stakes were formidably high.

Secondly, Mr Heath did not believe that a modern Conservative Party should fight an election battle aimed mainly against the trade unions. However skilfully the leadership might define the campaign issues, that was what the election would in his view become. A Party which repudiated the class struggle must not fight a class election. We must not treat the trade union leaders as enemies. Whether or not that was the right way to win an election, it was certainly no way to run a country.

Finally, truth was great and might still prevail. Mr Heath still believed passionately in reason as the governing force in politics. He had given the Party workers at Upton-on-Severn not a battle-cry but a reasoned lecture. Many times over the last two years the trade union leaders had come to Number Ten to reason with Ministers. Sometimes Ministers had come tantalizingly close to agreement with them. He would not despair of reason. One more meeting, one more initiative, one more exposition of the national interest – it must be right to persevere rather than despair.

The Prime Minister's decision was one which I regretted. But I respected greatly, and now respect even more the reasons for which he took that decision. In this mixture of feelings I was certainly not alone.

A lull followed. There were of course further talks with the miners. On 22 January Mr Heath had a substantial success at question time in the House of Commons. Under pressure he threw off his weariness and spoke as Prime Minister in terms which heartened his supporters. Two days later the Pay Board proposed that new machinery was needed to deal with the anomalies and unfairnesses which had inevitably been created in the first two stages of the incomes policy. They suggested a Relativities Board for this purpose. Everyone was at once alert to the possibility that the miners might be the first case to be referred to the new Board when it was set up. The Government was slow to agree, on the understandable ground that the new Board was supposed to deal objectively and calmly with those who had the strongest case, not in a rush with those who were causing the greatest trouble. In any case the miners were by now in a thoroughly unhelpful mood. Enraged by an announcement from Lord Carrington (the new Secretary of State for Energy) that coal stocks might permit us to move from a three to a four day working week, they went straight for a ballot among their members for a strike. This transformed the situation. It was clear that reason was not going to prevail.

On 26 and 27 January, while we were waiting for the result of the miners' ballot, I spent a strange, unreal week-end in the comfort of Ditchley Park. At this beautiful house in the heart of Oxfordshire had assembled an Anglo-American Conference which included a group of young American Congressmen. They had come to discuss problems of government in the broadest and most philosophical terms. With typical courtesy they refrained from any comment on the extraordinary condition of the country which they were visiting. The British participants included Sir William Armstrong, the Head of the Civil Service, who more than anyone else except the Prime Minister and Mr Whitelaw had carried the burden of the last few weeks. The atmosphere was Tchekovian. We sat on sofas in front of great log fires and discussed first principles while the rain lashed the windows. Sir William was full of notions, ordinary and extraordinary. On Sunday after lunch I went home with a notion of my own. It was clear that the miners would vote overwhelmingly for a strike. The Prime Minister had ruled out an immediate election. The Government could not for long withstand a strike. The best course might be to settle quickly with the miners and then go straight to the country for a new mandate, which would have to include a counter attack on trade union power.

On Monday morning no one liked my idea at the Liaison Committee. During the next two days Mr Heath made clear in several conversations how deeply he still disliked the idea of an immediate election. But he no longer had an alternative to offer. An election was the only weapon left in the Government's arsenal. Preparations were quietly resumed. There was no repetition of the great arguments of early and mid-January.

On 2 February the active Conservatives in Mid-Oxfordshire gathered in the British Legion Hall at Long Hanborough for a briefing conference. We were a new constituency, with new boundaries, new officers, new agent, new candidate. Although no election had been called, ninety people turned up on a fine Saturday to hear how an election would be fought. There was no warlike feeling against the miners and no oversimplification of the issues. On the scale of a single constituency it was an impressive gathering.

On Monday 4 February the Prime Minister began, though still not vigorously, to interest himself in election planning. We went through the draft manifesto less lackadaisically than before, but at the end there were big gaps in it still to be filled. It became clear that day that 81 % of the miners had voted for a strike. There was a further round of talks with the TUC at Number Ten; it lasted three and a half hours, and ended in deadlock.

It was not going to be possible to hang on much longer. British business was beginning to take fright. They were of course thoroughly seized of the dangers to themselves of the general wage explosion which would probably follow a surrender to the miners and collapse of the incomes policy – and which did of course follow, most destructively, a few months later. But that was hypothetical. What was actual was the disruption of industry which a coal strike would immediately produce. As usual actual fears prevailed over hypothetical fears. The employers' representatives were in no mood for further fight.

On the evening of Tuesday 5 February the Prime Minister dined at Pruniers with Tim Kitson and Francis Pym after a Cabinet Meeting. I joined them for a glass after dinner. Mr Heath explained more clearly than ever before his desperate worry about the size of the stake on the table. Everything which he had tried to do seemed at risk. No one pressed him that evening. Events had already taken over the argument.

The next day Sir Michael Fraser, Deputy Chairman of the Party, came round and gave Mr Heath an admirably clear and

fair account of the evidence which we had on public opinion and
of the technical factors. Obviously the Party would not go into
an election of this kind fully prepared. The massive campaign
guide, for example, with which the Party traditionally armed its
candidates, would have to be sent out in proof form. But we were
better prepared than our opponents. There were plenty of un-
certainties about the state of public opinion, which had clearly
become very volatile. But public concern over inflation and public
dislike of trade union power were well documented. Sir Michael,
a true professional, understood the nature of the decision which
the Prime Minister had to take. His presentation was most sober,
and he argued no case.

The Steering Committee met again that afternoon and made
more slow progress on the manifesto. It seemed that we had lived
for months with a hypothetical election, though in fact it was
only a few weeks. Early on the morning of Thursday 7 February
the decision was taken. We were off. The relief was very great.
There was an enormous amount to be done. There were Parliamentary questions to be answered that afternoon. The Prime
Minister had to broadcast. The manifesto had to be completed,
which was achieved briskly that afternoon with Lord Carrington
in the chair. The Prime Minister's election programme had to be
approved. We had been at work on these things for weeks, but
they all came to the point of decision on the same day. 'All in all
we are off the ground, in better shape than I dared to hope.'

The campaign was off the ground, but without me. Or, to be
more exact, I moved at once from a humble position in the
Commander's staff to an even humbler position in the front line.
I shall not write about the campaign itself because I know too
little about it. As Conservative candidate for Mid-Oxfordshire
I was in no position to judge, particularly as this was the first
election I had fought myself. Trundling in wet and wind from
village to village, from meeting to meeting, my supporters and I
read of the incidents which were said to be shaping the campaign.
Mr Barber made a controversial broadcast. Mr Powell managed
to manipulate a good many headlines. Mr Campbell Adamson
uttered a disobliging remark about the Industrial Relations Act.
It did not seem to us that these great metropolitan events made a
ha'porth of difference. But then as active campaigners each day
and evening we hardly watched the television or listened to the
radio. We were trying to make a local impact, and that is important, but we were curiously insulated from the real course of the

campaign in which we were taking part.

It all seemed to be going reasonably well. There was a great deal of Liberal noise and colour, but at second glance it was not particularly impressive. Their posters were not on private walls and doors, declaring the allegiance of an individual. They were flyposted on telegraph poles and signposts, declaring only that a Liberal team had passed that way. The local Labour Party was active with a rumbustious candidate, but did not seem to be making ground.

On Sunday 17 February I went back very briefly to head-quarters. The Prime Minister held a stocktaking dinner at Chequers. 'A cautious mood – we are just ahead in the polls, but the Liberals show much vitality, mortgages are a major worry, there may have been a slippage in the last forty-eight hours.' There was a worried discussion about the banks, which had, to the delight of the Labour Party, announced big profits during the campaign. 'What Lord C (Carrington) is really glum about is the fuel situation – entirely predictably. As someone said, the General Election is like another Christmas – three weeks of escapism while the stocks run down.'

Once again there was no pretence, in private or in public, that an election victory would by itself solve the coal dispute. There would have to be a negotiation with the miners at once. It would have to be based on the Pay Board's proposals for adjusting relativities. It would be a hard bargain. But at least after an election victory the Government would have strong cards in its hand. On 7 February it had had none.

Next Friday, 22 February, was the worst moment of the campaign. For the first time a national event made itself locally felt. 'A glum day till evening. We are cruelly savaged by Pay Board putting out entirely new figures on relative pay for miners, much more favourable to their case. EH retires in a cloud of stubborn and unconvincing negatives. A very difficult moment.'

Next day the Government recovered. It was clear by then that there had been no earlier slip which the Pay Board had just discovered. The two sets of figures, both correct, were calculated on a different basis. But for a few hours there had been confusion on a point which lay at the heart of the Government's case.

Four days later we lost the election. Not spectacularly, for we had a larger vote than Labour and only five seats less. Neverthe-less the calculation had failed. The week-end of fruitless discussion with the Liberals simply underlined the failure. Mr Wilson took office, and the country headed happily for several months of unreality, before the bills began to come in.

Could it all have been avoided? Yes, by abandoning the incomes policy. The political consequence of that would have been disastrous. The Government would have limped on in a broken-backed way for a year or so, probably under a different Prime Minister. The defeat at the hands of the miners and Lord Wilberforce in 1972 is crucial to this argument. In retrospect I do not doubt that we were right to advise against a second surrender on the same ground.

But could not the miners have been insulated from the main argument? Could they not have been clearly defined as a special case? It might in theory have been possible to declare the miners a special case as soon as it was clear that our oil supplies were at risk, and in any case would in future be enormously more expensive. Such a declaration would probably not have been acceptable at the time to the Government's supporters in Parliament or outside. It would probably not have been accepted at that time by the TUC, whatever they may have said later. The historian looking back can spot this brief opportunity before the struggle with the miners began in earnest. At the time the situation was not so clear cut. The forecasts about oil were wildly contradictory and full of 'ifs' and 'buts'. It was not until the New Year that the outline began to clear, and by the New Year that particular opportunity had slipped away.

Why, having resisted so long, did the Prime Minister finally agree to a February election? The political arguments set out in these pages had been used in his presence time after time during January but had not persuaded. He did not deny that our arguments had force. It was simply that in his mind other arguments prevailed. Why then the change? It was partly the deterioration of events, and in particular the lurch into a strike. It became almost impossible to see how a tolerable settlement could be reached without an election. But in my view, and I may be wrong, another argument was decisive. It had been there all along, but in Mr Heath's mind it grew steadily in strength. The more he studied the prospects, the more it emerged that oil rather than coal was the key. He had strongly practised and defended a policy of economic growth; it was now in ruins because of the oil price rise. The public expenditure cuts of December 1973 were only the first of the adjustments which would be needed. We were entering a period of lean years, perhaps many years of really harsh scarcity and impoverishment. The lean years would need new policies and a new vocabulary. There would have to be an end to promises. People would have to understand, because only with that understanding could their Government do what was needed. This was impossible for a Government elected in 1970, with policies and a vocabulary which were now out of date. The world had changed for Britain. Only a Government which had explained the change and been re-elected after that explanation could succeed.

I believe that Mr Heath would have liked this to be the main theme of the February 1974 election. In his own mind it *was* the main theme. It can be seen in his speeches and his broadcasts, and it constantly recurred in conversation. He disliked the election, he may for all I know regret it. I suspect that he would never have agreed to hold it at all on grounds of the coal dispute alone. It was the coincidence of the coal dispute with the disastrous change in our economic prospects which in the end clinched the argument.

CHAPTER NINE

HINDSIGHTS

When I got back to Number Ten on Monday 4 March, I found three sacks filled with papers in the middle of my office. Some kind person had already packed into them most of my own files in case there had to be a sudden evacuation. We had come in a hurry, we would leave in a hurry. The negotiations with the Liberals had petered out. Mr Heath was still Prime Minister, working in the Cabinet Room. He and Robert Armstrong and I talked of minor things in a matter of fact way. Then he said that he was sorry that it was all ending like this. It was a dark morning.

Dark for him, as I think he knew. Within a year he had lost another election and the leadership of his Party. Dark for those of us who had worked most closely with him. Not for our own prospects, which under our British constitutional system were not intimately linked with his, but dark, because a particularly bright period of our lives had come to an end. If I have not conveyed something of that quality, then this book has not been accurate. It is much easier to record the exasperation than the satisfactions; but the satisfactions were more important.

The satisfactions of working for this particular Prime Minister are hard to describe, and become harder as the years pass. That is why they should somehow be captured now, even though imperfectly. Most elusive, and perhaps most difficult for others to believe, was the wit, which was carefully concealed from the rest of the world, but was an essential part of his method of working. It did not take the form of verbal fireworks, let alone a string of jokes. The outrageous statement in a deadpan voice, the sardonic question, the long quizzical silence – these were hard for a newcomer to handle. Some never managed it, usually because they reacted nervously with a torrent of their own words. Those who found that they could slip into this idiom found it rewarding. It was more than just a flavour required to make hard work palatable. It marked an approach to life – tough, humorous, impatient of empty phrases. It was not surprising that Mr Heath found it particularly congenial to discuss the world with French and with Chinese leaders.

Allied to this was his sensitive kindness to those whom he knew well. Each of his immediate staff will have his own example of this. During the first part of my time at Number Ten, I was trying for selection as a Conservative candidate. Contrary to the general opinion, my job at Number Ten made this much harder, because of the publicity involved. The last thing which a constituency selection committee wants is to read in some London gossip column a prediction of its choice. The committee then shakes its collective head and goes the other way. In the end I was selected for a constituency where a much more prominent member of the Party was the front runner, so that he and not I suffered from the headlines. Twice before then I was involved in local contests which went badly and publicly wrong. The Prime Minister could do nothing whatever to help – except by saying the right thing to me at the right time. This was important, and he did it with great sensitivity, taking much trouble at times which were also troubled for him. This is a small example out of many which belong to other people.

There was a comradeship at Number Ten during that time. That is an overused word. By it I mean partly that there were very few quarrels or intrigues within the house. The atmosphere was wholly different from the strange enclosed bitterness described by Lady Falkender and by Mr Haines in their books about Mr Wilson's premiership. I am not saying here that our ideas were better or our ability greater, simply that we worked in greater harmony.

That was partly because of the Prime Minister's personality, but not entirely. It was also, I think, because we believed that we were part of an enterprise which was attempting something unusual and worthwhile. One of the difficulties in writing about politics is the debasement of language. In a sophisticated society like ours I could not possibly write about 'a great enterprise' without provoking a snigger. Every politician has written and made speeches about his own career in such terms until they have lost meaning. The next government which his own party will form is always going to be the one which finally sets the country to rights, restores it to its former glories, puts the 'Great' back into Great Britain, and the rest of it. Without therefore any wild hope of being credited, I would simply put on record that I, and I believe others, thought there was a real chance after 1970 that

Mr Heath and his colleagues would break out of inherited attitudes and make possible a sharply higher level of achievement by the British people. In short, there was a chance that they could do for Britain what Adenauer and Erhard had done for Germany, and de Gaulle for France. We saw that this was Mr Heath's passionate determination. Knowing his character and his record, we thought it might work.

A dark day also, then, for the country as a whole when the enterprise failed? In the short term, undoubtedly so. The period which immediately followed the general election of February 1974 was the worst in modern British politics. The quadrupling of oil prices and the success of the miners' strike put the country in great danger. The new Labour Ministers threw a few phrases at this danger, but in practice behaved as if it did not exist. Incomes policy was abolished, apart from an empty sentence or two in the first and most fraudulent version of the social contract. A disastrous wage explosion followed. Mr Barber's expenditure cuts of December 1973 were forgotten, and the budget deficit soared out of control. Britain's entry into the EEC was put at risk for party reasons. The experiment in power-sharing in Northern Ireland was allowed to collapse. At home and abroad the Government began to borrow recklessly to sustain a standard of life which the British people were no longer earning. Mr Heath and his warnings became, for the moment only, a subject of ridicule. The election campaign of October 1974 was on the Labour side a perfect example of the old corrupt style of politics. The promises and the deceptions did the trick, only just, but it was enough. The coming inflation at 25% and one and a half million unemployed were inconceivable – or if they were conceived it could only be in some nightmare vision of what future Tory policy might bring. Mr Wilson chose his moment skilfully. For in October 1974 reality had not quite broken through into the everyday life of the British voter.

In the longer term what will be the judgement on Mr Heath's administration? For some years to come it will be regarded on the left as a provocation, a period when because of accumulated mistakes and a failure by the Government to understand the working class, Britain was led into an internal struggle from which only the fall of the Conservative Government could save her. For them, 'confrontation' has already become a word of abuse, like 'appeasement' in the nineteen-forties, a word which you hurl at your opponent without pausing to consider if it has any meaning. No one need be particularly worried about this temporary version of history, because history will quickly dispose of it.

On the other hand, for some who began as sympathizers those years are construed as a period of aberration, of wilful wandering from the true principles of Conservatism. For reasons which I have already given I do not myself believe that this view is historically or philosophically justified. It has, however, a political danger. For it can (though it need not) lead to the conclusion that there were no huge difficulties in Mr Heath's way, and that he and his colleagues were in effect shipwrecked on their own heresies. If only they had understood the ideology of true Conservatism, it is argued, they would have found that the difficulties were entirely manageable. The huge rise in world commodity prices, culminating in oil, could have been accommodated without serious inflation if there had been strict control of the money supply. Given the same strict control, there would have been no need for an incomes policy in 1972. There would certainly have been no need to consult the trade unions about economic policy and so lurch towards the corporate state. There would thus have been no occasion for the miners' strike or for the premature election of February 1974. According to this analysis it is not true that Mr Heath ran out of luck, or that the obstacles were too great. He and his colleagues deserved to fail because they had no clear and consistent grasp of the correct line. The true star was all the time there in the sky, shining among the constellations, but the Government did not steer by it, and was therefore, as was inevitable, brought upon the rocks.

The danger of this theory lies in the implication that another Conservative Government will have a straightforward and not too difficult task if only it holds to its orthodoxy. The truth is different. Britain cannot be governed dogmatically or by the exercise of willpower. However well-founded the dogma, however strong the will, Britain can only be governed with the consent of people of widely differing opinions. A government which in its main decisions ignores the opinions of those who disagree with it is going to come to grief. This is not an argument for coalition, which is normally a bad form of government. It is an argument for taking account of the views of the Opposition and its friends in deciding the content and pace of government action. Only if this is done is the action likely to endure.

There is so much to be done in Britain which cannot simply be done by strength of will. There has to be a permanent shift of balance away from the public to the private sector. This involves a substantial and very difficult curtailment of government activity, in particular in the chaotic fields of housing and of subsidies to industry. There has to be an effective restraint on the power of trade unions, which is now privileged, undemocratic, and negative in its effect on the prosperity of trade unionists. There have to be sharp cuts in direct taxation. There has to be a political settlement in Northern Ireland which confounds the men of violence by showing that Protestant and Catholic can run the province together. There has to be a determination to make the best instead of the worst of Britain's position in Europe. There is nothing new about these imperatives. If they could be met simply by an exercise of will, then Mr Heath and his colleagues would have met them between 1970 and 1974 more completely than they managed. The willpower of Ministers is not in itself enough.

This is not to deny the mistakes of that period. Of these two stand out. The single-minded pursuit of growth involved acquiescence in the growth of the money supply during 1972 and part of 1973 beyond the limits of likely production. This made it more difficult to cope with the explosion of world prices, and more difficult to restrain wage settlements through incomes policy, particularly in the public sector, where in theory but not always in practice, the Government has the greatest power as the ultimate employer. One does not have to believe that monetary policy is the alpha and omega of economic management to accept that criticism. It was made at the time and it proved to be valid.[1]

The other main failing was in communication. An earlier chapter has discussed this at length. In this failure Mr Heath's Government was not very different from others in recent times. All governments have suffered from the growing and justified disillusionment in Britain with the way the political system works. Having aroused expectations, politicians have had to explain why these could not be satisfied. Having moved into ever more complicated fields of government action, they have failed to find simple and accurate words to describe those actions. Having

[1] It is worth noting nevertheless how the terms of the argument shifted. In 1972–3 many reputable economists worried mainly about M.1, the narrower definition of the money supply which excludes many types of deposit. By this standard the Conservative Government performed reasonably. Since then the emphasis has changed to the wider definition known as M.3. It was on this definition that the big increase occurred in 1972–3.

blamed their predecessors for everything that went wrong, they have had to argue that there are after all world forces which the British could hardly influence but which affected the livelihood of everyone in Britain. Having run out of skill or out of luck, they have tried to put the most favourable interpretation on increasingly unfavourable events. Mr Heath and his colleagues came into office with the strong will to avoid these traps. But it was not until too late that the Prime Minister put into full practice his belief that bad news was best presented bleakly, that it was possible to reach behind the interest groups to a national interest, and that on a political as well as a patriotic calculation, there should be an end to promises. The few weeks of an election campaign were not enough. It was a mistake not to make the break in style and content before there was any question of an election.

But when these mistakes (and others beside) are properly weighed, they will probably turn out to be a small part of the story. All governments make mistakes and pay a price. What distinguishes Mr Heath's Government is something different. He devoted himself to starting a new chapter of achievement in this country. The quiet revolution was not a phrase to be turned at a Party Conference and forgotten. It was the purpose of his political career. He and his colleagues had studied at length in opposition how it was to be achieved. They set to work on it in earnest. On the whole they were not successful. Some things they failed to achieve at all. Much was achieved in part, and then demolished by their successors. But the analysis was not wrong. The weaknesses they tried to cure were real enough. Indeed they have become much worse since they left office.

Inflation, unemployment, lack of investment, overweening trade union power, industrial and agricultural stagnation, weakness in Europe and the world – the old problems, now aggravated, will have to be tackled all over again. The years of Mr Heath's Government should be regarded as a necessary first attempt, the rough work of pioneers.

There was another period not long ago when politicians had to decide whether to insist on or whether to defer a policy requiring much effort by the British people. Suppose that the Conservatives when they entered the National Government in 1931 had insisted that the country should re-arm. Suppose that a major defence programme had been set in hand, despite massive protest from the Opposition Parties and the trade unions. The British people were not ready to re-arm. They still believed that peace could be secured without pain or sacrifice. So suppose that after a few years the Conservatives lost office and the new aircraft and warships were scrapped by a Labour Government which believed, against the evidence, that the old phrases about collective security and the League of Nations were still enough. By 1939 the British people might have looked back with regret to the re-arming government of 1931 saying 'They made mistakes, but at least they had the courage to do what was right. It would have been better to listen to them. Now under different leadership it has to be done again.' The parallel, though fanciful, is worth a thought. It may explain why Mr Heath often drew larger audiences and commanded greater general respect after his defeat than when he led his Party.

If it is right to look on Mr Heath's Government as the first attempt at a necessary but highly difficult process, what can we learn about the prospects for the next attempt?

The international risks can soberly be assessed as less frightening. There will be surges and falls of commodity prices. Behind these will be the continuing pressure of the developing countries for more favourable conditions of trade. Because the industrialized world has an interest in the stability of the remainder it will in practice, after much huffing and puffing, continue to make gradual concessions to these pressures. The main change will probably not come about from dealings between governments. It will occur because several developing countries will continue by natural competition to elbow British industry out of traditional markets at home and abroad as they learn to manufacture competitively. But it is not likely that primary producers of any other commodity will wish or be able to follow the example of the oil producers in 1973, and impose a drastic political penalty on consumers. It is conceivable that the oil producers themselves might repeat the action, perhaps on a less drastic scale, if the Palestine dispute drags on; but countries like Kuwait and Saudi Arabia now understand clearly the wider risks of an oil price policy which damages most those in the West who, despite all exasperations, remain their necessary friends. We in Britain are moreover protected for fifteen or twenty years by North Sea oil from the direct effects of politically inspired price rises should they occur – though of course we remain vulnerable to the secondary effects if our main customers in Western Europe and North America were hard hit.

In addition, though this is less certain, it looks as if the governments of the main Western countries have learnt something from the panic of the winter of 1973. The oil price rise struck the EEC at a bad moment. It had not digested the entry of Britain, Denmark, and Ireland. It was caught unprepared. Britain in particular had bad trouble at home. Each country manoeuvred in the Middle East for its own interests. There was only the vestige of a common policy towards the Palestinian dispute. I am not sure that if there were a similar crisis the Community would perform as well as its friends would like. The member states have still not equipped the Community with the diplomatic and economic bargaining power needed to protect Europe's interests in the Middle East. But it is reasonable to hope that we would be spared the humiliations of 1973.

In the wider Western world the same is true. One need not put absolute faith in all the communiqués of all the international meetings which have taken place since 1973. That indeed would be a strain on the mind. But it is reasonable to believe that the United States, Japan and Western Europe are slowly learning that as part of the framework within which their economies compete with each other there are common interests which justify constant talk and occasional common action.

But there must be a sombre qualification. If the industrialized nations have learnt to co-operate just a shade more effectively, Britain's voice in that co-operation has grown fainter. This is partly because of our poor economic performance. It is even more because of a failure of statesmanship.

Having decided painfully over many years to become a member of the European Community, we have failed to take advantage of that membership. It is not entirely our fault. The Community as a whole has been slow to exploit its opportunities. It could be a major civilian power, exercising diplomatic leverage through its commercial and financial strength in every continent. If it learned to use its strength, it could be a major force for peace and for the protection of the interests of its member states. But the Community hesitates unhappily in the doorway. This is a new venture. There has never before been a purely civilian power, using loans and tariffs and debt settlements to further its diplomacy without control over armies, navies and airforces. There has never been a partnership of states acting together abroad while retaining most of their sovereignty at home. These are new concepts to be worked out, new habits to be formed. The rest of the world waits, like an audience waiting for the appearance of a star actor who has forgotten his entrance cue. They know that an important moment should have arrived, but all they hear is shuffling and muttering off stage, and the occasional agitated twitch of a curtain. Or, to change the metaphor, the EEC is a prototype. Like many prototypes it is expensive, imperfect, and hard to manufacture. Nevertheless it is the most hopeful advance in international relationships in this century. One cannot travel in countries outside Europe without realizing the power for good which here lies hidden.

The tragedy is that Mr Heath would have been the right person to release this power. He had the talents and the reputation to persuade his fellow Prime Ministers to set aside minor differences and work effectively towards a common foreign policy. He certainly had the wish to do so, for he had expressed it long before in his Godkin Lectures at Harvard. As the Prime Minister who had through many hazards taken Britain into Europe, he had a great stock of personal credit. But Britain did not enter the Community until New Year's Day 1973. The opportunity came too late.

In Britain itself the changes since February 1974 are confused. The actual condition of the country, if measured by economic comparisons with other industrial countries, has further deteriorated. The North Sea oil is producing its good effect on the balance of payments, but despite fluctuations we still have a rate of inflation sharply higher than that of our competitors, and this is the single most powerful fact about the British economy today. For it has led to a reluctance to invest, an inability to increase production, a savage increase in internal and external debt, and a rate of unemployment likely to remain high at a time when our competitors with lower rates of inflation are able to create a larger number of new real (i.e. profitable) jobs. The next effort to revive Britain will have to begin from a much less favourable starting point.

In addition there is now less confidence in the British political system. As one government after another fails to meet expectations, confidence withers further. While individual Members of Parliament are often respected and even liked, they find that the reputation of Parliament itself has declined. There is less interest in the comings and goings of party politics, less belief that the result of any particular general election is crucial. There is a much greater resentment now among practical people at the instability which our system imposes on their lives. They see in Germany and the United States democratic political systems which give the voter a real choice, but which do not involve abrupt and destructive changes of domestic policy every four or five years. France and Italy have the enormous disadvantage of large Communist Parties built into their political system. We do not have this penalty, but increasingly our own politics in their effect on ordinary people seem more like the politics of France and Italy, and less like those of the more successful democracies, which once looked to us as a model.

It follows that, next time, part of the revival of Britain must be a revival of Parliament, as the centre of our political system. This was not something to which Mr Heath and his colleagues paid much attention. It is not true that they deliberately neglected Parliament, but they were not particularly concerned with its reform. Indeed one of the damaging paradoxes of recent British politics is that politicians have been eager to reform every institution except their own. The smallest change in the procedures of the House of Commons is harder to carry through than the nationalization of a great industry. The constructive reform of the second chamber, as opposed to the trimming of its powers, has hung fire for most of this century. Parliament has become less and less concerned with the intelligent discussion of real issues. The party manoeuvres which are its daily concern seem less and less important to its electors. Parliament has moved or been moved some distance away from the centre of the nation's life.

This is bad for democracy, but it is also bad for governments. The experience of Mr Heath and his colleagues illustrates the point. The Labour Opposition played the parliamentary game to the utmost. They paid little regard either to consistency or to the needs of the country as recently defined by themselves. For example they knew and had said that Britain needed to enter the EEC, to overhaul her trade union system, and to hold back excessive wage claims. Yet when the Conservative Government which they opposed acted in these directions, they shouted murder. The next Labour Opposition, unless the system changes, is likely to behave in the same way. The results may be just as damaging to confidence. However resolute and skilful a Government, its task will be enormously complicated if it faces an Opposition which reacts violently against all its actions and promises to repeal them when it has the chance.

Since 1974, the Conservative Party has come to see that it

loses under this system. For Conservative Oppositions in the last twenty years have not been as ruthless as Labour Oppositions. Europe again is an example. In May 1967 Mr Heath asked his Party to vote for the Labour Government's intention to apply for membership of the EEC. In June and again in November 1977 Mrs Thatcher asked her Party to vote for the Labour Government's Bill providing for direct elections to the European Parliament. It is impossible to imagine a Labour Opposition actually whipping its members in this way to support a Conservative Government measure. In the same way, despite powerful misgivings, the Conservative Opposition under Mrs Thatcher did not seek to destroy the different stages of the Government's incomes policy between 1975 and 1977. Between 1972 and 1974 the Conservative incomes policy was under constant and ruthless attack from Labour.

Some Conservatives naturally enough react to this imbalance by saying that in Government and Opposition the Party must stop being feeble. It is the duty of an Opposition, they say, to oppose and this may mean putting the immediate national interest second to the Party's fundamental purpose of regaining office. But this is a downhill path. If the political parties in this country further increase the distance between each other then our political system will further deteriorate. The noise, the instability and the destructiveness will increase. We shall drift even further away from the instincts of our constituents. Sensible people will be even more inclined to call down a curse on both our houses.

The right answer is to give Parliament responsibility, and bring it back to the centre of affairs.

There are two particular needs as regards the House of Commons. The first is to enable the electorate to choose a House which actually reflects their views. The second is to equip the House to resume the control of the executive which it has largely lost, more through its own inaction than through the depredation of governments.

The detailed proposals are well known. There needs to be a sharp curtailment of new legislation, releasing talent and time for its real job. The House of Commons needs to reassert its control over Government spending on the lines compellingly set out in a recent pamphlet by Mr Edward du Cann. In place of the present untidy 'cat's cradle' of Select Committees there should be a small number of powerful Select Committees in each main field of policy, competent to take evidence from senior civil servants and outside experts as well as from Ministers. The same Committees should be able to take evidence on the need for and content of any new legislation before it is actually introduced in the Chamber. The proceedings of the House and its main Committees are now broadcast on radio so that our constituents can hear what we are at, and tell us what they think of it. This is a big step forward. Last but not least, the House of Lords should, while keeping roughly its present powers, be transformed into an effective revising chamber by a system of democratic election, which could also provide for the inclusion in that House of the directly-elected Members of the European Parliament.

These ideas have been elaborated by others of much greater experience than myself. They amount to a reform considerably less drastic than Parliament has imposed on, for example, local government or the National Health Service. Yet the need for Parliamentary change is a good deal more obvious than the need for change in these other institutions.

In 1977 people throughout the European Community were asked what they thought was the most important function of national parliaments. In Britain most people thought the control of the spending of public money was Parliament's most important job, whereas in France it was thought to be the passing of new laws. The House of Commons has got its wires crossed and is listening to the wrong message. We pass a multitude of new laws. We no longer effectively control what the executive does and spends.

Reform of Parliament would not be against the interests of Government. On the contrary an essential part of the argument is that good government is handicapped if Parliament is irresponsible. When Members of Parliament are starved of facts and of the opportunity to influence policy in time, then partisanship has a field day. Over the long term the quality of government suffers. The philosophizing Mayor of Tours, Monsieur Royer, has coined a telling phrase: '*la politique politicienne*' – the political activity in which only politicians are interested because it has no link with actual life. Politicians drift into this activity when they have nothing real to do. They develop their own vocabulary. They work each other up into artificial passions. They raise barriers between themselves and practical people. This has been the curse of French and Italian politics for many years. The House of Commons and the British people generally have prided themselves that by comparison they are of the earth, earthy. In fact we have let our parliamentary system drift into the bad habits which we have criticized in others.

So, the next government which tries to take over where Mr Heath and his colleagues left off will have to work hard to repair the damage done recently to our influence in Europe and to the effectiveness of Parliament. Further neglect of either task would be most harmful in the medium and long term. But of course the central and immediate question which people ask is different. Whether or not they accept that it is desirable that the power of the trade unions and the role of government in Britain should be restrained, they ask whether this is possible. Have the internal forces which destroyed the last effort lost their force? Or are they still waiting in readiness to destroy the next?

No one can honestly be sure in advance, but there are some sober reasons for hope. There has certainly been a sweeping intellectual change in Britain since 1974. This goes far wider than the swing towards monetarist economics. The shift away from collectivist thinking can be measured in the universities and colleges, for example in the increase in the number of organized Conservative students. It can be measured in new publishing houses and new organizations for the defence of causes and interests which till recently were passive and silent. It can be measured in the media; it can be measured even in the Labour Party.[1] This intellectual groundswell is something different from by-election results or public opinion polls. When I was an undergraduate in 1949–51 there was a similar movement of opinion. In 1968–70, despite all the Conservative by-election victories, there was not. As anyone who recalls the 1970 election campaign will know, Mr Heath and his colleagues won that election against and not with the tide of intellectual opinion. This made their feat more remarkable, but it also made their task more difficult.

There is nothing tangible about intellectual opinion. There is no precise or visible obstacle against which Ministers bang their heads when that opinion is opposed to their inherited philosophy. But anyone who has held high office knows what such opposition means. The people talking round a common-room table, an

---

[1] I once heard Denis Healey say that, whatever the merits of the late Anthony Crosland's arguments for public spending, he forgot that the money had actually to be found from somewhere. This remark sounds banal to anyone unacquainted with the modes of thought of the British Labour Party. In fact it marks a great leap forward.

editor's desk, a television studio, a company boardroom, are through the strange interweavings of British life more in touch with each other than they know. They have different ideas for society, but they edge towards a common view of what is actually possible, and they have the means to express it. A politician, moving rapidly from one of these rooms to another, meets different people of different political persuasions saying the same sort of thing about a particular situation. He is bound to be impressed. When this general comment runs in favour of what he is trying to do, he must be encouraged. The next government which tries to shift the balance of power away from the state and away from the trade unions will find, at least initially, that the general comment is on its side.

It will be said that this advantage is nice but not decisive. If Mr Heath and colleagues lacked an intellectual groundswell on their side, that was not the reason for their eventual defeat. They lost because, despite the most strenuous efforts by the Prime Minister, the trade unions turned against the Government's economic policy, and in particular its attempt to limit wage increases. The trade union leadership, backed by the Labour Party, allowed the miners to break the Government. This had nothing to do with intellectual groundswells, with dons or journalists. It had to do with the brutal exercise of trade union power. For what reason, it is asked, can anyone suppose that this would not happen again?

Not all the evidence is reassuring. The trade union leaders still offer economic ideas which work against the interests of their members. The honeymoon period of 1974–5 when their advice was most willingly accepted by government, was also the period when government policy had the worst effect on trade unionists' standard of living. This is no coincidence. Though there has been hopeful change in some individuals the British trade union leadership is still in the grip of outworn concepts which more successful trade unions overseas abandoned long ago. They still under rate the dangers of inflation, and the merits of profit. Despite their own experience, they still overrate the virtues of planning and the competence of the state. They are still wedded too intimately to one political party. They are too sensitive to criticism. Without wishing to be tyrants they believe that the trade union movement needs privileges and powers which most people in this country find repugnant. They are still painfully unrepresentative of their members.

Yet in spite of all this they can still usually rely on a loyalty inherited from the past. Their critics can point to a long line of opinion surveys stretching back over many years which show that a majority of the electorate, and often a majority of trade unionists, hold views quite contrary to those which trade union leaders express on their behalf. Yet the traditional feeling of solidarity is still strong. Workers, including the new white-collar trade unionists, are often willing to join in industrial action against private employers or the public, even though it is called by leaders in whose selection they took no part, in defence of claims with which privately they disagree, in pursuit of a socialist philosophy against which they regularly vote. How long this illogical solidarity will last is anybody's guess. Cracks are beginning to show, but a powerful habit takes time to break. The Conservative Party under Mrs Thatcher's leadership has stressed that Conservatives who are eligible should join a trade union and take full part in its work. It would be a great mistake to forsake that approach, for it is crucial. Neither Government nor Parliament can change the attitudes of the trade union movement. Its members can, but only if they exert themselves on behalf of reality.

Reality will be the chief ally of the government which takes up the task which Mr Heath had to abandon. A new sense of reality is beginning to touch some of the old arguments. There is the argument that excessive wage claims threaten jobs. That was just an argument when unemployment was low, and serious unemployment confined to a few areas far from London. Now unemployment is everywhere, and the argument has become real. There is the argument that if private firms and individuals are discouraged beyond a certain point they will no longer be able to produce the wealth needed to finance schools and hospitals and the other hungry giants of the welfare state. Not long ago, that was a theoretical argument because Governments were still able to finance welfare programmes out of a reasonable level of private prosperity. Now it is a real argument as new hospitals stand unopened, and thousands of teachers are without a job. The facts of life are Tory, as the policy document, 'The Right Approach' said. This obviously does not mean that the Conservative Party will from now on win every election. We live in a country whose working class by and large hold conservative views yet are suspicious of the Conservative Party. But it does mean that the closer the country comes to reality the easier it is to apply Con-

servative policies.

Easier, but still not easy. Change in Britain comes much more slowly than intellectuals suppose. Much depends on the art of communication between Government and people. Government will have to appeal continuously and convincingly over the heads of organized interests and pressure groups. Government will itself have to stay firmly moored alongside reality.

This is the last and most important point. Mr Heath's most lasting contribution to British politics may well have occurred in the last months of the premiership. It may have come indeed at the very moment when his efforts and achievements seemed to dissolve and collapse around him. He was faced with the certainty that the British people would after the oil price rise suffer a severe cut in their standard of living. In the winter of 1973 he believed that this setback might amount to a catastrophe. He could have tried to gloss over this prospect. He could have manoeuvred for time or talked about temporary difficulties. He could in fact have played the hand as Mr Wilson played it a few months later. He decided otherwise. In his mind the conclusive argument in favour of an election early in 1974 was not the miners' dispute. It was necessary to hold to the incomes policy, but this was not the central fact. The central fact was that the whole landscape had been changed by the quadrupling of oil prices. To cope with the new problems the Government needed a new mandate following an election in which the new prospects had been plainly expounded. Of course it did not turn out like that. There were ambiguities about the miners' dispute in the Government's election campaign. But it was on the whole a campaign without promises, a bleak honourable affair, an exercise in presenting reality. It almost worked, even in 1974.

Now reality has come that much closer, and politicians again have a choice. They can continue in the old ways. They can issue fat manifestos packed with promises. They can seek out every opportunity to abuse each other. They can treat the electorate as the dimmer disc jockeys on radio and television treat their audience. Everyone does well, there are prizes for all, the world is infinitely sentimental, and every utterance from the platform is greeted with organized and lunatic applause.

If that is the choice which politicians make, then the broad outcome is fairly easy to predict. For several years before he became an Ambassador Mr Peter Jay developed in *The Times* with much force the argument that our political system was incompatible with national success or even survival. In particular he believed that politicians were bound to respond to short-term pressures, particularly in favour of full employment, which could not be reconciled with sound policy. These pressures, or rather the failure to resist them, would eventually lead to ruin. Mr Jay wrote in public what many intelligent people have been saying in private ever since the suffrage became universal. It is too soon to be sure that they are wrong. But there is nothing inevitable about this process. The quality of political debate and political leadership has not slipped downhill all the way. It is not true that politics have become steadily more debased as the suffrage has widened. On the contrary, as more and more people became able to vote during the nineteenth century, the standards of political life improved. Anyone who reads the biographies of two great Conservative Prime Ministers, the younger Pitt and Lord Salisbury, finds that the hundred years which separated them had done a power of good to the intelligence and integrity of the political system.

In our century, the improvement stopped, and then went into reverse. For many reasons both intelligence and integrity suffered. Expectations were allowed to rise far ahead of reality, and politicians found expectations an easier currency to handle. But this cultivation of unreality is not inevitable. Today it is not even good politics. Patronizing optimism is now a loser, for promises are not believed. Bad news is best exposed, not camouflaged. Sir Winston Churchill proved this point in the desperate but politically simple circumstances of war. It would be too much to claim that Mr Heath proved the same point in peace. Nevertheless that is the main lesson which personally I carried away from my not very important service in Number Ten, and the main reason why I do not accept Mr Jay's despair. The evidence is still confused. It is not certain that our politicians will make the necessary changes in their methods of work and habits of thought and speech; but there is now a chance. It is certain that they must do so if our democratic system is to continue. In particular it is certain that they must do so if they are to regain the respect or hold the acquiescence of the electorate.

INDEX

INDEX